AM
MAPGUIDE
Michael Middleditch

CW00541849

CONTENTS

PENGUIN BOOKS

INTRODUCING THE CITY

IMPRESSIONS

Intimate and full of contrasts this lively city which has over 100 canals is full of surprises. Not jammed with lorries and cars or as polluted as many other European cities are, it is an ideal place for walking or bicycling. The tram system is excellent too, perfect for whisking you very quickly to other parts of the city.

VILLAGE OF ISLANDS

The site on which Amsterdam now stands was once a boggy empty marshland - in fact Holland means 'hollow land'. In the early 13th century by building dykes and polders the watery landscape was contained and a small fishing village emerged where the Amstel river flowed into the river Ij - pronounced Y! The place where they dammed the Amstel and diverted it into canals was Dam Square (A4 16): to this day the city still retains the name 'Aemstelle Dam' - Amsterdam. Alongside the canals, houses were built, supported by wooden piles driven into the firmer sub layers. As the Middle Ages drew to a close Amsterdam had become a great port, the centre of a very lucrative herring industry: the merchants had found a way of preserving the fish for export. They were traders with panache, and bankers - especially after the decline of Antwerp in the 16th century when there was a large influx of Portuguese Jews seeking refuge from oppression. Catholic and part of the Holy Roman Empire, which was under Spanish rule until the Reformation, Amsterdam gained independence in 1581, after continuous guerilla warfare and William of Orange's rebellion. The city then became a part of the Netherlands Province: William was later shot in Delft by a fanatical catholic.

THE GOLDEN AGE

With its new-found freedom the city became the financial capital of the world before London. The Dutch built their civilisation on bank money - the promise to pay in coin of certain value if required: merchants and traders borrowed money to build ships, trade expanded and with the arrival of the Dutch East India Company and the West India Company in 1621 Amsterdam was the concourse of trade, banking, art and cartography. The three great canals the Prinsengracht, Keizersgracht and the Herengracht were extended to the north and east to accommodate the wealthy merchants: a part of the Herengracht renowned for its opulence is known as the Golden Bend (H2 19). During this period there were several trade wars with England when Oliver Cromwell tried to ensure that only English ships carried imports: the English were snubbed when the Dutch hero Admiral de Ruyter sailed up the Thames and captured the *Royal Charles,* the British flag-ship - whose coat of arms is proudly displayed in the Rijksmuseum. It is undoubtedly true that the English learned many things from the Dutch and that jealousy was the motive for the fighting!

ART AND CARTOGRAPHY

With the overthrow of Spanish rule more refugees found a haven in Amsterdam. Artists flourished in the tolerant environment, artists like Rembrandt and Vermeer. The city at that time was a model for civilisation: the streets were clean and lit with oil lanterns, unlike Paris and London which were not very sanitary places. With the advent of world trade in the 17th century it became a centre not only for commerce but for mapmaking: many of the world's most brilliant cartographers published their great maps and atlases in Amsterdam, men like Willem Blaeu and his son Joan: they had strong links with

the Dutch East India Company which enabled the to get the latest information. The Dutch had no riv. in cartography for many years.

ANGLO-DUTCH LINK

Overseas, the Dutch had established an importa colony in America; it had been bartered from t Indians for $24 worth of beads and ribbons, and w called New Amsterdam. The English under the Du of York (later King James II) took the colony a renamed it New York. James II was not so popul when he became King and reverted to Catholicis so he was ousted and his daughter's Dutch husba William of Orange - who was a Protestant - becar King William III of England in 1689.

OCCUPATION

Taken by the Prussians in 1787 and then eight yea later by the French, the city was past its glorio heights when in 1808 Napoleon installed his broth as Emperor of the new Netherlands Republic whi included Belgium. After the defeat of Napoleon Waterloo the country reverted to Dutch rule und William I; later, in 1832, Belgium broke away become an independent kingdom. The great feat engineering and construction of the North Sea Can in 1876 then heralded a revival of fortunes; this ar the discovery of a wealth of diamonds in Sou Africa, which to this day has made Amsterdam th world's leader in diamond cutting. Neutral durir the First World War, the country had no choice whe Hitler invaded in May 1940 and occupied the ci until only a few days before the surrender in 194

LIVE AND LET LIVE

Amsterdam with its cobweb of canals is still th capital city of the Netherlands, sharing responsibili with The Hague, which is where the governme resides. Its liberal policies towards drugs, rac religion and sex have made the city an attraction young people, but there is a lot more to Amsterda as I am sure you will discover. It is unique and certainly is not a threatening city at all. It is alway interesting whether you look up at the gable ston with their colourful depictions, cruise along th canals, visit a museum, or meander through the re light district. I am sure there is something for a tastes in Amsterdam...*Gezellig.*

LANGUAGE

Dutch is the language of the Low Countries. It is derived from three German dialects spoken along the North Sea coast, and is very closely linked with the Flemish language of Flanders in the northern part of Belgium. It is somewhere between English and German, although there is a French connection influenced by the Protestant Huguenot exiles who lived in the Jordaan district.

AX MUSEUM   Not on map area.
Amsterdam Arena, Arena Boulevard 3.
Take the metro or train to Bijlmer station
and walk up the road. This museum tells
: illustrious story of the great Dutch football team,
ginning with 3D animation and ending in a film
:atre. You can also get a tour around the new all-
it high-tech stadium, which has a sliding roof
i holds 50,000 people, and is one of the largest
diums in Europe. *Open Daily 9.00 - 18.00, check
ening time match days (usually Sundays).*   *Charge*

LARD PIERSON MUSEUM   **A6 16**
de Turfmarkt 127. The archeological museum
iated in a former bank building containing Greek,
ruscan, Roman and other antiquities from 4000
C to 1000 AD. There are some interesting scale
idels of the Giza pyramids and the Temple of
us at Olympia: perhaps the highlight is a full-
:e Greek chariot. *Tues 10.00 - 17.00, Sats,
ns, and Holidays 13.00 - 17.00.*   *Charge*

MSTELKRING, MUSEUM   **C3 16**
idezijds Voorburgwal 40. Atmospheric like a Pieter
Hooch or Vermeer painting, this canal-side house
extremely evocative of the 17th century 'Dutch
ilden Age'. On the fourth floor in the attic is the
iden Roman Catholic church - in 1578 after the
formation Catholics were not permitted to worship
blicly. Fine paintings, sculptures, furniture, ornate
verware etc.   *Mons - Sats 10.00 - 17.00,
ndays and Holidays 13.00 - 17.00.*   *Charge*

MSTERDAM HISTORISCH MUSEUM   **H5 15**
ilverstraat 92. Situated in a former 17th-century
phanage you can discover through objets d'art
i photos the history of the city. The glass-roofed
vil Guard Gallery - a public passageway in
ytime - exhibits some enormous paintings.
ljacent to the museum is a lovely courtyard, the
:gijnhof (a former convent), a serene retreat from
: bustle of the nearby shopping sector; it contains
: oldest house (Het Houyens Huys) in Amsterdam.
ins - Fris 10.00 - 17.00,
ts, Suns and Hols 11.00 - 17.00.*   *Charge*

NNE FRANK HUIS   **F3 15**
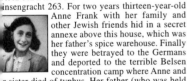
insengracht 263. For two years thirteen-year-old
Anne Frank with her family and
other Jewish friends hid in a secret
annexe above this house, which was
her father's spice warehouse. Finally
they were betrayed to the Germans
and deported to the terrible Belsen
concentration camp where Anne and
r sister died of typhus. Her father (who was held
Auschwitz) was the only survivor, and in 1947
: was able to get Anne's inspirational diary of the
ars in hiding published. This museum today
esents a warning against racialism of any
scription. The museum is very popular so it is
visable to get there early.
ien Daily September - March 9.00 - 19.00.
iril - August 9.00 - 21.00.*   *Charge*

VIODROME   Not on map area
:hipol Centre. Situated in Schipol Airport, follow
: signs from the train station. The museum of
itch aviation with many historical Fokker aircraft,
:at flight-simulators and a space department.
iily April - September 10.00 - 1700.
:tober - March Tues - Fris 10.00 - 17.00.
ts & Suns 12.00 - 17.00.*   *Charge*

BEURS VAN BERLAGE   **B3 16**
Damrak 277. Architecturally one of Amsterdam's
most interesting buildings. This was the original
stock exchange dating from 1903 and designed by
Holland's most famous architect Hendrik Berlage.
The building is now used for concerts and to display
an exhibition on the history of the stock exchange.
From the clock tower there is a magnificent view
over the city. *Tues - Suns 10.00 - 16.00.*   *Charge*

BIJBELS MUSEUM   **G6 15**
Herengracht 366. The Bible museum in two adjacent
atmospheric canal houses built in 1662 with the
main hall ceiling painted by Jacob de Wit and a
peaceful garden. The collection includes
archeological finds from Egypt and the Middle East
and many models. *Mons - Sats 10.00 - 17.00.* *Charge*

EROTIC MUSEUM   **C3 16**
Oudezijds Achterburgwal 54. Five floors of boys-
girls-night-out material situated in one of the main
streets of the 'Red Light' district.
Daily 11.00 - 01.00, Fris & Sats. 02.00.   *Charge*

JOODS HISTORISCH MUSEUM   **D1 20**
Jonas Daniël Meijerplein 2-4. Located in the area
that was Jewish Amsterdam are four former
synagogue buildings dating from the 17th-18th
centuries and linked with a modern steel and glass
structure. There are some marvellous examples of
Dutch-Jewish art, and works by Charlotte Saloman
who died in Auschwitz at the age of 26. Diamonds,
the Holocaust, a beautiful marble ark and a kosher
coffee shop serving local delicacies are some of
the features.   *Daily 11.00 -17.00. Charge*

MULTATULIMUSEUM   **H2 15**

Korsjespoortsteeg 20. Dedicated to the
19th-century writer Eduard Dowes
Dekker, whose leaning sculpture stands
on a bridge a few blocks away. This
was his house and it is filled with
memorabilia. *Tuesday 10.00 - 17.00,
Saturday 12.00 - 17.00.*   *Free*

NEDERLANDS FILMMUSEUM   **C4 18**
Vondelpark 3. A museum, cinema, film archive and
a café restaurant all combined in a lovely 19th-
century pavilion near the entrance to the park. The
interior of the cinema is the Cinema Parisien (the
first cinema in Amsterdam) saved and restored.
*Exhibitions Mons - Suns 12.00 - 19.00. The cinema
opens Mons - Suns 16.00 - 21.30 see press. Charge*

NEDERLANDS PERSMUSEUM   **G2 23**
Cruquiusweg 31. Spanning four centuries of print
this is the archive of the Dutch press. Cartoons,
objects, advertisements, photographs etc.
Mons - Fris 9.00 - 17.00, Sats 9.00 - 13.00.   *Free*

NEDERLANDS SCHEEPVAARTMUSEUM H5 17
Kattenburgerplein 1. A truly interesting museum
that charts the maritime past of this great seafaring
nation, located in a warehouse which looks more
like a palace and dates from 1656.
Superb models of ships up to the
20th century; some huge action
canvases in monochrome pen and
ink by Willem van de Velde: if
you look closely you can see him
being rowed right into the battle
making his sketches. There are some marvellous
old maps on display and the instruments the
surveyors and cartographers used at that time.
Anchored alongside is the *Amsterdam,* a replica of
an early East India vessel. *Tues - Suns 10.00 - 17.00,
Mondays Middle June - Middle September. Charge*

REMBRANDTHUIS, HET   D6 16

Jodenbreestraat 4-6. Rembrandt lived and worked in this house from 1639-58. This is where *The Nightwatch* was created and where the artist spent his most happy years with his wife, Saskia and later with his mistress. In the 70-seat auditorium his life and work will be explained to you; then you move on to see over 250 prints of his graphic work - the largest collection in the world.   *Monday to Saturday 10.00 - 17.00, Sundays and Public Holidays 13.00 - 17.00. Charge*

RIJKMUSEUM MUSEUM   F5 19

Stadhouderskade 42. The most important collection of Dutch historical art in Holland, including *The Nightwatch* by Rembrandt which dominates the Gallery of Honour on the top floor. With paintings

by the exquisite Frans Hals, Vermeer, Jan Steen's *Woman at her Toilet* - a 17c painting of a woman putting on her stockings. Huge pen and ink canvases by the great maritime painter Willem van de Velde; furniture, jewellery, Delft earthenware, Chinese porcelain, room settings of canal houses, these are but a few examples of the varied collection which you will need at least an afternoon to see. *Daily 10.00 - 17.00.*   *Charge*

ROYAL PALACE (KONINKLIJK PALEIS)   A4 16

Dam Square. Built in 1648 as the town hall when the city was the most important trade centre in the world, it became a palace in 1808 when Louis Napoleon became King of Holland and moved in. The interior is sumptuous, particularly the Burgerzaal (citizen's hall) with its floor of marble hemisphereal inlaid maps. Sculptures, paintings by Ferdinand Bol and Jacob de Wit, furniture, clocks etc. *Daily July - September 12.30 - 17.00.*   *Charge*

SEX MUSEUM   B2 16

Damrak 18. An amusing alternative museum with a collection of erotica including photographs, objects, statues, and cartoons from Roman times to 1960: not really a rip off compared with some such enterprises! *Daily 10.00 - 23.30.*   *Charge*

STEDELIJK MUSEUM of MODERN ART   E6 19

Paulus Potterstraat 13. Renowned for holding the most important collection of modern art in Holland, the museum illustrates the development of the visual arts of the 20th century, particularly after 1945. Includes works by Chagall, Picasso, Mondrian, Man Ray, Malevich: this museum is a complete contrast to the emotional experience of the nearby Van Gogh museum. *Daily April - September 10.00 - 18.00, October - March 11.00 - 17.00.*   *Charge*

THEATER MUSEUM   G3 15

Herengracht 168. In the splendid Bartolotti House built by Hendrik de Keyser in 1618, although you enter the museum through the so-called White House. There is a beautiful 18th-century spiral staircase with plasterwork decoration and some lovely murals by Jacob de Wit to look out for. The collection includes costumes, models, photos, posters, stage sets and a miniature theatre.   *Charge Tues - Fris 11.00 - 17.00, Sats & Suns opens 13.00*

TORTURE MUSEUM   B2 16

Damrak 20-22. I am a gentle soul so you would not get me near this one, ever since I saw *The Captain from Castile* these things give me the creeps. No doubt some might enjoy the experience of the inquisition chair and the guillotine etc. *Daily 10.00 - 23.00.*   *Charge*

TRAMLIJN. MUSEUM   B4

Amstelveenseweg 264. Run by a group of amat enthusiasts the museum has a large collection historic rolling stock dating from 1910 to 1960, only from Holland but also from Berlin, Prag Vienna and Bonn. Your visit takes you for a minute six-kilometre ride from the museum to Amsterdamse Bos (Wood). *April - Oct, Sundays and Pub. Hols, 10.30 - 17 July & August Saturdays as well.*   *Cha*

TROPEN MUSEUM   C4 :

Linnaeusstraat 2. Housed in a palatial building t was constructed in 1923, the Tropical Museum v transport you to the tropics: you can stroll throu a realistic reconstruction of an Arab casbah with the noises you might expect, walk round courtyard of a Javanese house, get caught ir thunderstorm in the African savannah, and i makes you hungry there is also a restaurant Eke which serves authentic tropical snacks and even meals. Compared with other museums the inter of this building is extremely photogenic. *Monday - Friday 10.00 - 17.00, Saturdays, Sund and Public Holidays 12.00 - 17.00.*   *Char*

VAN GOGH MUSEUM   E6

Paulus Potterstraat 7. Few art museums in the wc can compare with this one. It really is an experien to see a human being's short tortured tragic li story and development so clearly depicted by own art. Vincent amazingly only took up paint properly in 1883; he died in 1890: his paintin were initially in sombre dark colours, and as y move round the museum you see the colour bu in front of your eyes. As well as his paintings there are drawings, letters and his own collection of Japanese prints which clearly made an impact on his own painting style. Other paintings by contemporaries and friends of Van Gogh are also on display including works by Gaugin, Monet, Toulouse-Lautrec, Signac, Is; Israëls and Emile Bernard. This is one muse that you should not miss. *Monday - Sunday 10. 00 - 17.00.*   *Char*

VAN LOON MUSEUM   A3 :

Keizersgracht 672. A classical Dutch canal ho built in 1671 with all the furnishings that recoll the famous Golden Age of Dutch history. The ar Ferdinand Bol, one of Rembrandt's pupils, or lived here. Objets d'art, ornate furniture, and o sixty Van Loon family portraits. *Friday - Monday 11.00 - 17.00.*   *Char*

VERZETSMUSEUM   G1

Plantage Kerklaan 61. The museum of the Du Resistance to the German Fascist occupation duri the Second World War. The exhibits show dilemma the Dutch people had to face at that tin Emphasis is put on the "Februari Strike" and underground press. *Tuesday - Friday 10.00 -17.C Saturdays, Sundays & Pub Hols 12.00-17.00. Cha*

WILLET-HOLTHUYSEN MUSEUM   C2 :

Herengracht 605. A 17th-century canal house clo by Rembrandtplein furnished in 18th-19th-centu Rococo style. The first floor has a magnifice ballroom and an immaculate garden which almc backs on to the famous It Disco, while downsta you get a glimpse of life in the scullery. *Monday to Friday 10.00 - 17.00, Saturday and Sunday 11.00 - 17.00.*   *Char*

PLACES OF INTEREST

ARTIS - ZOO G1 21

Plantage Kerklaan 38 - 40. This is a great zoo - one of the best, with over 6000 animals, a fascinating park to walk round, and a really unique combination of zoo, Botanical Gardens and Planetarium. It has a 19th-century atmosphere with appropriate historic buildings and yet the approach modern, giving the animals as much space as possible, and they are improving on this with the annexation of the wasteland by the side of the Entrepotdok canal. Many species can be seen including: polar bears, lions, tigers, elephants, gorillas, chimpanzees, seals, giraffes, and the best tropical birds - parrots etc. - I have seen outside the Rio zoo. There are man-made objects here too, scattered among the many lovely trees, including sculptures of animal figures and a squatting Buddha. Special mention should be made of the Goat Rock made in 1941 and inhabited by alpine ibexes. The aquarium is superb with sharks, piranhas and a view of underwater life in an Amsterdam canal. Recommended for everyone and you can arrive by boat from Central Station on the Artis Express or just take tram 9. *Daily 9.00 - 17.00, Mondays the Planetarium opens at 12.30.* *Charge*

CHURCHES AND RELIGIOUS BUILDINGS

Nieuwe Kerk A4 16
Dam. Dating from the 14th century and reconstructed several times after fire, the Dutch Kings and Queens swear their oath of allegiance here. In the apse is the tomb of the Dutch naval hero Admiral de Ruyter which was completed in 1681. Renowned for its splendid organ and concerts.

Noorderkerk G1 15
Noordermarkt 48. Located in the Jordaan district, this church was designed like a Greek cross by Hendrick de Keyser, who died two years before the church was completed in 1623.

De Krijtberg G1 19
Singel 448. A Roman Catholic church built in 1881 with two steeples. De Krijtberg or chalk-hill is a nickname which derives from the fact that a chalk merchant's house previously stood on the site.

Mozes en Aäronkerk D1 20
Waterlooplein 205. Completely dominating the Waterlooplein, this church was built in 1841 with twin towers in a similar style to St.Sulpice in Paris these towers are identical and are made of wood unlike the towers of St.Sulpice.

Oude Kerk C3 16
Oude Kerksplein 23. Situated in the Red Light district this was the first parish church in Amsterdam and it can be clearly seen on the early maps of the city dating from the end of the 13th century. The vault ceiling paintings have survived the years, having been covered with prussian-blue paint.

Portugees Israëlietische Synagoge E1 21
Mr. Visserplein 1. Now a national monument, this building dates from 1675 when Jewish refugees from Spain and Portugal sought sanctity in the Netherlands. Modelled by the architect on the Temple of Solomon in Jerusalem.

Westerkerk F3 15
Westermarkt. Claiming to have the tallest tower (280ft. 85m.) in Amsterdam, it is capped by the orange Imperial Crown of Maximilian. This is yet another church designed by Hendrick de Keyser. You can go up the tower if you feel young and fit enough to attempt the climb. Rembrandt's much-painted son Titus is buried in this church.

THE ZUIDERKERK, AMSTERDAM (LOOKING UP THE GROENBURGWAL) CLAUDE MONET

Zuiderkerk C5 16
Zuiderkerkhof 72. Now offices of the city planning department, this former church designed by the architect Hendrick de Keyser in 1603 is still a prominent landmark. From June to September you can climb the tower. It was the subject of two paintings by the impressionist artist Claude Monet.

HEINEKEN BROUWERIJ H6 19
Stadhouderskade 78. This tour round the old brewery for 18-year-olds and over has the added attraction of not only free beer but snacks - the admission fee is donated to the Red Cross to make it even more worthwhile. The tours are in groups and it is best to obtain your ticket in advance to save waiting around. *Monday - Friday at 9.30 and 11.00. Between 1st June and mid September extra tours at 13.00 and 14.30, and on Saturdays in July and August 11.00, 13.00 and 14.30.* *Charge*

MADAM TUSSAUD A4 16
Dam 20. The famous wax museum has a Dutch emphasis, with a 17th-century canal stroll and a view of Rembrandt and Vermeer at work etc. There are also currently famous people and rock stars. *Daily 10.00 - 17.30.* *Charge*

MAGERE BRUG D3 20
The so-called Skinny Bridge is Amsterdam's most photographed bridge. Made of wood, this drawbridge can be raised to allow boats and barges through.

MUNTTOREN A1 20
Muntplein. The lower section was part of a gateway through the old city wall; the top part, the clock tower, was added by Hendrick de Keyser in 1619. It was given the name Mint Tower when it was used in 1672 to mint gold and silver coins when the city was temporarily cut off from its monetary supply.

NEW METROPOLIS G3 17
Oosterdok 2. Where the Ij Tunnel drops under the water you will see a spectacular green-copper building like a sinking ship; this is the Technology Centre. The sloping roof plaza is free for everyone to clamber up and gives a fine view of Amsterdam from the top. The centre is about having fun with technology with interactive exhibitions, computer games to challenge you, and a theatre and cinema. *Daily 10.00 - 18.00, Saturday to 21.00.* *Charge*

WAAG, DE C4 16
Nieuwmarkt 4. This old turreted castle-like city gate dates from the end of the 15th century. It later became the city weigh house, a prison and a place of execution. Today it houses a very nice restaurant called *In de Waag*.

SHOPPING

Wandering through the old streets of Amsterdam which are relatively free of traffic makes shopping a pleasure in this historic city. With only a few department stores, small individual boutiques of every kind are in abundance. C & A, a Dutch company, has one store in central Amsterdam, compared with three shops in London's Oxford Street.

Kalverstraat (A5 16) is completely pedestrianised and is one of the most crowded places to shop. Walking northwards across Dam Square you enter Nieuwendijk (A3 16) which seems to get tattier with more jeans and souvenir shops.

In contrast Rokin (A6 16) has trendier fashion boutiques, jewellers and the most fantastic cigar shop I have ever seen - P.G.C.Hajenius: the interior of this shop is well worth seeing alone, it is truly majestic and the aroma is sublime, I always think cigars smell better before you put a light to them. In the shop there is a bar serving tea or coffee and various alcoholic beverages.

The Museum Quarter along Pieter Cornelisz Hooftstraat (E5 19) and Van Baerlestraat is where many of the smart designers have shops - it is the fashion centre of Amsterdam.

Leidsestraat (F2 19) is the place to find some very good shoe shops like Ecco etc. and the fashion store Metz & Co.

The Jordaan is always an interesting area to walk through, with the canals and its picturesque narrow streets dotted with cafes, bars and many artistic shops selling jewellery and specialised clothing - new and secondhand. This area is a favourite for young people, students and artists.

Opening hours are usually Monday 13.00 - 18.00 (department stores open at 11.00).
Tuesday to Friday 9.00 - 18.00 (Thursday 21.00).
On Sundays many shops in the centre of the town are open from 12.00 - 17.00.

It should be noted that many small shops will not accept credit cards, so you might be asked to get cash from a cash machine round the corner which of course you will instantly pay the interest on!

SUPERMARKETS

The biggest and most well-known supermarkets are the Albert Heijn chain. Most of these you will find on the maps in this atlas: their best shop with a vast selection and a good delicatessen counter is Food Plaza (H4 15), located behind the Royal Palace. Another to recommend is situated at the rear of the Heineken Brewery (C1 26) - this is the Dirk van den Broek supermarket.

Stores and Shops

DE BIJENKORF B4 16
Situated in the centre, right on Dam Square, you will find this large department store: five floors selling almost everything. It is the largest store in Amsterdam, smaller yet comparable to Printemps in Paris. Designer clothing and its own quality label and an excellent restaurant.

CONCERTO C3 20
Taking up the space of about three shops, this is an excellent place to browse for both new or secondhand CDs and records; you can listen before you purchase.

MAGNA PLAZA H4 15
The magnificent old neo-gothic Central Post Office built in 1899 has now turned into a hive of over forty separate boutiques. On the lower floor music lovers will find the well-stocked Virgin Megastore.

MAISON DE BONNETERIE A1 20
Very French as the name suggests, and with the balustrades, balconies, domed roof and a quaint lift the image is complete. Old-fashioned expensive, principally clothes, but nice.

METZ & CO. G2 19
Although owned by Liberty's of London it does not have the same cosy atmosphere, it is more modern and sparsely shopfitted. The store, which dates from 1891, sells furniture, cosmetics, clothes, glassware, Liberty fabrics etc. The cafe-restaurant on the top floor has fine views over Amsterdam and is a must, try it for late breakfast or tea.

DE SLEGTE A5 16
A very interesting bookshop in Kalverstraat, one of the largest bookshops in the city, selling both new, remaindered and secondhand books.

VROOM & DREESMANN A1 20
A very reasonably priced department store with fine selection of almost everything. La Place, the self-service restaurant, is always tempting, the tables on several floor levels provide seating which many people may not realise is available.

Art and Antiques

Leading down to the Rijkmuseum is Nieuwe Spiegelstraat (H3 19). This street is lined on both sides with art and antique dealers. Furniture clocks, Delftware, sculpture, glass, modern art curios, jewellery and other objets d'art are all to be found in this unique street.

Markets

ALBERT CUYP C2 26
Amsterdam's most well-known general market vegetables, clothing etc. and the traditional Dutch organ. *Monday to Saturday 9.30 - 17.00*

ANTIEKMARKT DE LOOIER E6 15
An enclosed reasonable quality antiques market *Saturday to Wednesday 11.00 - 17.00.*

BLOEMENMARKT H1 19
Probably Amsterdam's best-loved market and certainly the most colourful - the Floating Flower Market. *Monday to Saturday 9.30 - 17.00*

BOEKENMARKT H1 19
The secondhand book market which is situated at the bottom of Spui. *Friday 10.00 to 18.00*

DAPPERMARKT D4 23
A very good general market in the Indonesian sector. *Monday to Saturday 9.00 to 17.00*

KUNSTMARKT THORBECKEPLEIN B2 20
The art market on Thorbeckeplein: paintings drawings, ceramics and sculptures of high quality *Sundays 10.30 to 18.00, not in winter.*

NIEUWMARKT C4 16
Antiques on *Sundays May to September* and organic produce on *Saturdays both 9.00 - 17.00*

NOORDERMARKT G1 17
Next to the Noorderkerk. Secondhand general goods *Mondays 9.00 - 13.00*. On *Saturdays from 9.00 - 16.00* an organic farmers and bird market.

POSTZEGELMARKT H5 19
Stamps and coins, on the island in front of the Nova Hotel. *Wednesday & Saturday 13.00 to 16.00*

WATERLOOPLEIN D6 16
This is the flea market: army surplus, leather bric-a-brac, Indian hash pipes, secondhand clothes and junk too. *Monday to Saturday 9.00 - 17.00*

PARKS AND GARDENS

STERDAMSE BOS See key map PAGE 10
good way to visit the Bos (Wood) is to combine
with a trip on one of the Trammuseum's historic
ms (see Page 4). A Roosevelt-style project
lising the unemployed in the 1930s created the
s - the largest park in Amsterdam. In the
rthern part of the wood the Bosbaan, a canal,
ich is approximately two straight kilometres,
sses it diagonally, and is used for swimming
d boating. There is a buffalo and bison reserve,
atersports centre, and several nature trails.

TRIX PARK PAGE 25
se to the RAI Centre this is a beautiful park
often visited by people who are hoteled in
northern part of the town. It has a wonderfully
ceful walled garden, a feature worth a visit.

RTUS BOTANICUS F2 21
is is the Botanical Gardens, now part of
sterdam's University. These beautiful gardens
re originally laid out in 1682 and sponsored
the East India Company who used them to
tivate and study the plants and seeds they
ught back from afar, to see if they were of
mmercial value. In the Palm House there is a
cas (palm fern), 400 years old and still going -
world's oldest potted plant! In the new Hot
use see the *Victoria Amazonica*, a huge waterlily
ich can hold a large baby.   April to September,
ns - Fris 9.00 - 17.00, Weekends 11.00 - 17.00.
tober to March closes 16.00.   Charge

OOSTERPARK PAGE 22
Young people staying at the Arena Hostel will no
doubt be glad to find some peace and quiet in
this pleasant park with its sweeping lake. This
park is particularly nice in spring when it is
covered with sheets of colourful tulips. During
the summer months there are pop concerts.

SARPHATIPARK PAGE 26
Banker Samuel Sarphati's monument dominates
this small park which with its lake and ducks
gives the impression of more rural surroundings.
The park was laid out in the 19th century and
Sarphati was an instigator: he developed the idea
of more open spaces in poorer urban areas. Being
close to the Albert Cuyp market it presents a
pleasant place to rest and enjoy a sandwich.

VONDEL PARK PAGE 18
Created in 1865 and named after Holland's great
17th-century poet Joost van den Vondel, whose
seated statue can be seen topping a monument in
the north east section of the park. It is a very
nice English-style park with lovely trees and
shrubs, lakes, a bandstand, and it is ideal for
rollerblading and jogging, being over a mile in
length. There are animal enclosures with horses
and cows and I am sure I saw a llama; an open-
air theatre with free concerts during the summer
months and the Filmmuseum (see Page 3), which
has the *Vertigo Café* - a very good place to stop
for a beer or coffee.

RESTAURANTS AND CAFÉS

sterdam has a very wide choice of International
isine so you will have no need to go Dutch
ery night! It is worth remembering that many
the good restaurants take last orders around
out 10 o'clock. Because of the Dutch East India
nnection there are quite a few Indonesian
staurants and they are renowned for their
jsttafel' which is almost a national dish; it is
ry colourful and consists of many small dishes,
ually offered in a two, three or six person menu.
ality varies so choose wisely!

e Dutch are great beer drinkers, and they also
nk the strong jenever (a kind of sweet gin)
ually contained in stone bottles and served in
all glasses. Wines from all over the world are
ailable; for good value try the South African.

BATROS E2 15
uated in the atmospheric friendly Jordaan district
s is a small family-run restaurant that serves
cellent seafood dishes: lobster, oysters etc.

FÉ AMERICAIN E3 19
most on the Leidseplein the terrace bar of this
-deco café with its high ceiling is worth a visit
en if you only go for a coffee.

SA DI DAVID G1 19
amed ceilings and a romantic atmosphere make
pizzas - which are cooked in wood-fired ovens
nd the pasta a real treat.

JAREN. CAFÉ B1 20
unpretentious café come designer bar with a
ry popular patio terrace that backs right on to
Amstel; renowned for its salad buffets.

KROON. GRAND CAFÉ B2 20
erlooking Rembrandtplein from the north side.
e entrance is obscure: go up the stairs and you
ter this high ceilinged Grand Café. Good food
d a fine view if you get a window seat.

SAMA SEBO F4 19
The 'rijsttafel' served here will not be a let down.
This is one of the best and the most spacious
Indonesian restaurants in Amsterdam and it is not
expensive if you choose your food carefully.

SANCERRE F4 15
A theatrical art-deco-style interior in an intimate
domed room. French/Dutch specialities.

SEA PALACE F3 17
A large floating Chinese/Indonesian restaurant
anchored in the Oosterdok with great views of
Amsterdam, and accommodating unbelievably 900
persons on three floors. An exotic place with the
decor and ladies in cheongsans to match, the food
is basically Cantonese cuisine.

SLUIZER C3 20
There are two restaurants with interior design
reminiscent of a Parisien brasserie; one serves all
kinds of fish dishes and the other serves meat.

DE TUIN F2 15
A brown-café much frequented by local artists in
the heartland of the Jordaan, a good place to soak
up the atmosphere. Occasional jazz.

D'VIJFF VLIEGHEN G6 15
The name 'Five Flies' may put you off, however
this is a world-famous restaurant and it is quite
expensive. Panelled walls and Rembrandt etchings
give this place an old world atmosphere. The
cuisine is Dutch/French...Elvis once ate here!

WINTER GARDEN B4 16
This is a wonderful atrium room in the centre of
the Krasnapolsky Hotel. Try their lunch buffet.

ZINC...ET LES DAMES A4 20
Reasonably priced French regional cooking and
good wines in a former canalside warehouse with
a ground-floor bar.

ENTERTAINMENTS

For information on day-by-day events going on in Amsterdam it is best to buy the monthly English edition of *"What's On"* which is obtainable at bookstalls or from the Amsterdam Tourist Offices (see page 28). Daily newspapers carry listings on current peformances and there is also a free entertainments newspaper *"Uitkrant"* which is usually found at bookshop entrances.

Concert Halls

BEURS VAN BERLAGE   B3 16
Damrak 213   ☎ 627 0466
The original stock exchange with its magnificent interior is now the resident home of the Netherlands Philharmonic Orchestra.

CONCERTGEBOUW   G2 25
Concertgebouwplein 2-6   ☎ 671 8345
The Grand Hall of this auditorium which was built in the 1880s is world-famous for its magnificent acoustics; it is a place where many superb performances have been recorded for posterity, it is also the home base of the Royal Concertgebouw Orchestra. During summer months there is a sponsored progamme of musical events all reasonably priced. The hall is not only a venue for the classics but also it often plays host to many of the world's great jazz artists. There is a smaller hall for chamber music works.

IJSBREKER   E6 21
Weesperzijde 23   ☎ 693 9093
By the Amstel with a terrace café overlooking the river, this is a place where avant-garde and contemporary music has found its platform.

OTHER CONCERT VENUES
Baroque and modern music concerts are often held in the famous church buildings of Amsterdam, such as Oude Kerk, Nieuwe Kerk, Westerkerk and the English church in the Beginjhof (H6 15). For locations see page 5.

Opera and Ballet

FELIX MERITIS   F1 15
Keizersgracht 324   ☎ 623 1311
Originally built in 1787 the building's canal frontage features a neo-classical palladian façade. During the 70s the theatre became known as the "Shaffy", the name of the avant-garde theatre company. Today it often features modern and experimental ballet groups.

MUZIEKTHEATER   D1 20
Amstel 3   ☎ 625 5455
Stuck with the name "Stopera", both opera and ballet are featured in this vast complex which also includes the Town Hall and was built in 1988, despite public opposition to the demolition of the medieval houses in what was the old Jewish quarter of Amsterdam, hence the nickname! The theatre today is the largest in the Netherlands and is where both the Netherlands Opera and the Netherlands Dance Theater companies reside: both these classic art forms can be viewed without paying over the top prices for a seat. If you do go to a performance you could combine it with a meal in the *Dantzig* café-restaurant which is situated on the corner of the complex and has good views of the Amstel river.

STADSSCHOUWBURG   F3
Leidseplein 26   ☎ 624 2:
A traditional neo-renaissence-style theatre bu in 1894 right on the square (Leidseplein), whi features opera, ballet as well as serious and ligh theatre productions from touring companies. T National Reisopera perform here too.

SOETERIJN - Tropen Museum   C4
Linnaeusstraat 2   ☎ 568 85
This can be found in the Tropen Institute. progammes generally feature non-western dan groups from around the world.

GRACHTENFESTIVAL - Canal Festival
Every year during August the Prinsengracl and Keizersgracht canals become the scene c a magical festival of music which lasts for fou days: some performances are in the histori houses that line the canals, including the state Felix Meritis Theater, while other concerts ar in the open air, on canal barges.

Theatres

There are many small theatres tucked away Amsterdam. The street called Nes (A5 16) cou almost be called the theatre district with theatr like **FRASCATI** and **DE BRAKKE GRONDE** whi have Dutch language programmes but occasiona have dance groups. Here are a few that ha programmes that might be of interest to you.

BOOM CHICAGO   F2
Leidseplein 12   ☎ 423 0ſ
You can dine and drink in this theatre (beer a margaritas in pitchers) during the showtime: dinr starts at 18.30. The performance usually at 20. is by an eclectic group of American improvisato comedians from the Windy City.

DE KLEINE KOMEDIE   B1
Amstel 56   ☎ 624 05
An 18th-century theatre that features some Engli language shows and occasional pop stars a classical performers in concert.

KONINKLIJK THEATER CARRÉ   D4
Amstel 115-125   ☎ 622 52
An imposing 19th-century circus building with classical façade right on the Amstel. It is a lar theatre; because of its shape it is preferable get more central seats. Programmes feature ope ballet and touring American shows. In the foy you can see posters featuring some the stars wl have appeared here such as: Marlene Dietric Shirley Maclaine and Liza Minnelli.

MARIONETTEN THEATER   D4
Nieuwe Jonkerstraat 8   ☎ 620 80
Amsterdam's fairy-tale classical marionette thea which has a programme of Offenbach and Moz operas - no language problems here!

Ticket Agencies

Tickets for most venues can be obtained from t
AUB TICKETSHOP   F3
located on the Leidseplein right next to t Stadsschouwburg Theatre.
AUB Uitlijn *(9.00 - 21.00)*   ☎ 020 621 12
Or from:
AMSTERDAM TOURIST OFFICES see Page 2

Cinemas

Amsterdam's first-run commercial mainstream multi-screened cinemas are situated close to the Leidseplein (F3 19). The city also has many art houses and one superb unique cinema that has no rival anywhere. Many of the cinemas have interesting cafés attached. Films are hardly ever dubbed into Dutch, but shown in the original language with subtitles. It is advisable especially at weekends to book in advance, note that programmes change on a Thursday. Here are a few cinemas that might interest you.

BELLEVUE / CALYPSO Cinerama　　　E3 19
Marnixstraat 400 and 402　　　☎ 623 4876
Separate and comfortable cinemas often used for premieres, they share the same box office.

CINECENTER　　　　　　　　　　　E2 19
Lijnbaansgracht 236　　　　　☎ 623 6615
Features a wide international selection of films.

CITY　　　　　　　　　　　　　　F3 19
Kleine Gartmanplantsoen　　　☎ 623 4579
A modern seven-screen establishment with a large frontage just off the Leidseplein.

DESMET　　　　　　　　　　　　　F1 21
Plantage Middenlaan 4a　　　☎ 623 3434
An independent cinema with art-deco design and a café, late Saturday night and Sunday afternoon gay and lesbian films.

FILMMUSEUM　　　　　　　　　　　C4 18
Vondelpark 3　　　　　　　　☎ 589 1400
The National Film Theatre of Holland shows films from all countries, of all descriptions, including silent films with a piano background. On fine summer evenings there are often free open-air screenings on the terrace overlooking the park.

KRITERION　　　　　　　　　　　F4 21
Roetersstraat 170　　　　　　☎ 623 1708
Opposite the university with interesting selections of programmes, and a bar with atmosphere.

MOVIES, THE　　　　　　　　　　E5 13
Haarlemmerdijk 161　　　　　☎ 638 6016
Not much to look at from the front, inside it is a renovated 1920s art-deco-style cinema with the seats to go with it; adjoining is a café/restaurant.

PATHÉ DE MUNT　　　　　　　　　A2 20
Vijzelstraat. Next door to the Tuschinski with 13 screens (2438 seats), and a façade designed by the designer of the Cité de la Musique in Paris, Christian de Portzamparc - opening spring 2000.

TUSCHINSKI　　　　　　　　　　　B2 20
Reguliersbreestraat 26　　　☎ 626 2633

Opened in 1921 this cinema was the dream of a Polish jew called Abraham Tuschinski. It has been open every day since. A combination of architecture and all the allied arts, it is beautiful. In the 20s and 30s there was a room upstairs with a balcony called the *Cabaret La Gaîté* which provided an evening entertainment and a dance floor. Great entertainers such as Josephine Baker and Maurice Chevalier appeared there: during the Second World War it was destoyed by fire when some German officers were having a party; it is now a second cinema. The designs are a mixture of art nouveau and art-deco; door handles, panelling, toilets, wallpaper, lighting, the entrance carpet in one piece made to the original design in Morocco (this is the second one), chairs in the VIP room from the Holland-America line...it is a marvel. The main theatre is about 24 metres across and has a wooden balcony and the original Wurlitzer organ on the left of the stage. Tuschinski spared no expense to make this theatre. He died in Auschwitz...This is the memorial to the "Napoleon of the Duvelhoek".

Jazz in Amsterdam

BIMHUIS　　　　　　　　　　　　D5 16
Oudeschans 73-77　　☎ 625 5685
The place for very modern and experimental jazz often frequented by American legendary groups.

BOURBON STREET　　　　　　　　F3 19
Leidsekruisstraat 6　　☎ 623 3440
The name infers jazz of the New Orleans variety but this is not always the case at all. Larger than the Alto Café round the corner.

CASABLANCA　　　　　　　　　　D3 16
Zeedijk 26　　　　　　　　☎ 623 1361
A cosy pub-like atmosphere for aficionados. Often features one of Holland's best tenor saxophonists Hans Dulfer - the father of Candy!

JAZZ CAFÉ ALTO　　　　　　　　F3 19
Korte Leidsedwarsstraat 115　☎ 623 3249
A long bar featuring bebop and modern jazz. A good place to enjoy a beer and listen.

> **LATIN** Lovers of the music of Latin America - Brazil, Cuba etc. - will find tropical sounds in these two places: **CANEÇAO** (F2 19) and the **BAMBOO BAR** (F3 19).

Discos

ESCAPE　　　　　　　　　　　　B2 20
Rembrandtplein 11　　　　　☎ 622 3542
A vast cavernous Saturday-night-clubbing venue.

IT　　　　　　　　　　　　　　C2 20
Amstelstraat 24　　　　　　☎ 625 0111
A glamourous venue, with Thursdays and Saturdays specifically for gays.

MAZZO　　　　　　　　　　　　E4 15
Rozengracht 114　　　　　　☎ 626 7500
A hip place that plays underground house music.

MELKWEG　　　　　　　　　　　E2 19
Lijnbaansgracht 234a　　　　☎ 624 1777
A multi-media centre often featuring live acts, and a mix of hip-hop and house.

ODEON　　　　　　　　　　　　H1 19
Singel 460　　　　　　　　☎ 624 9711
Three floors of varying sounds in elegant settings.

PARADISO　　　　　　　　　　　F4 19
Weteringschans 6-8　　　　☎ 626 4521
Friday nights are great here, live music too.

ROXY　　　　　　　　　　　　A1 20
Singel 465　　　　　　　　☎ 620 0354
A converted cinema with good sound and a gay night on Wednesdays.

> **HOLLAND CASINO - LIDO**　　　　F3 19
> Max Euweplein 62　　　　　☎ 620 1006
> Legal roulette, black jack and slot machines, with dance and cabaret shows in the Lido disco.

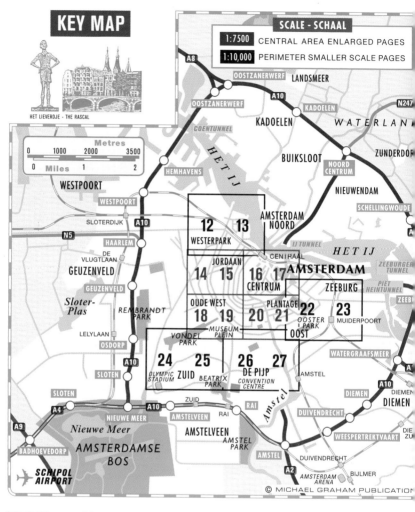

KEY MAP

HET LIEVERDJE - THE RASCAL

SCALE - SCHAAL

1:7500 CENTRAL AREA ENLARGED PAGES
1:10,000 PERIMETER SMALLER SCALE PAGES

Metres
0 1000 2000 3500

0 Miles 1 2

© MICHAEL GRAHAM PUBLICATION

1:7500 1 CENTIMETRE TO 75 METRES
approximately 8¹/₂ inches to 1 mile

1:10,000 1 CENTIMETRE TO 100 METRES
approximately 6 inches to 1 mile

225 METRES EQUAL 246 YAR

300 METRES EQUAL 328 YAR

METRES	0	100	200
	0	75 **A**	150

ENGLISH	The maps are divided into 225-300 metre squares with divisions of 75-100 metres indicated in the border.
NEDERLANDS	De kaarten zijn verdeeld in vierkanten van 225-300 meter met verdelingen van 75-100 meter in de kantlijn.
FRANÇAIS	Les cartes sont divisées en carrés de 225-300 mètres de côté, avec divisions de 75-100 mètres indiquées en bordure.
DEUTSCH	Die karten sind in karees von 225-300 quadratmeter unterteilt 75-100-Meter-Unterteilung ist am Rand markiert.
ITALIANO	Le mappe sono suddivise in 225-300 metri quadrati con divisione di 75-100 metri indicate nel margine.
ESPAÑOL	Las cartas están divididas en cuadrados de 225-300 metros, con divisiones de 75-100 metros indicados en el margen.

ENGLISH - NEDERLANDS - FRANÇAIS - DEUTSCH - ITALIANO - ESPAÑOL — LEGEND

HOSPITALS
Ziekenhuisen
Hopitaux
Krankenhäus
Spedali
Hospitales

Onze Lieve
Vrouwe Gasthuis

POLICE STATION
Politie
Gendarmerie
Polizeiwache
Polizia
Comisaría

PB

POST OFFICE
Postkantoor
Bureau de Poste
Postamt
Ufficio Postale
Correos

PHARMACY
Apotheek
Pharmacie
Apotheke
Farmacia
Farmácia

HOTEL
Hotel
Hôtel
Hotel
Albergo
Hotel

GRAND HOTEL
KRASNAPOLSKY ■

CHURCH OF SPECIAL INTEREST
Interessant Kirken
Eglises intéressants
Sehenswerte Kirchen
Chiese di Interesse
Iglesias de Interes

OUDE KERK

SHOPS
Keus van Winkels
Choix de Magasins
Einige Läden
Scelta di Negozi
Selección de Tiendas

DE
BIJENKORF

DISCO or DANCE HALL
Disco of Dans Zaal
Disco ou Salle de Danse
Disko oder Tanzsaal
Disco o Sala di Danza
Disco o Salón de Baile

Exit ★

SUBWAY STATION
Ondergrondse Station
Station de Métro
U-Bahnstation
Stazione di Metropolitana
Estacion de Metro

Nieuwmarkt

TRAMLINE and LINE NUMBER with STOP
Tramlijn en lijnnummer met halte
Tram lignes et arrêt
Strassenbahn mit haltstelle
Tram linea con fermata
Tranvia linea con parada

—20—●

BUS NUMBERS
Autobuslijn nummers
Autobus numéros
Busstrecke nummern
Autobus numeri
Autobus numéros

BUS *TRAM*
20 120 126   9

JAZZ CLUB
Jazz Club

CASABLANCA ★

TOURIST INFORMATION
Toeristen Informatie
Informations Touristiques
Touristenauskünfte
Informazione Turistiche
Información Turistica

MUSEUMS
Museums
Musées
Museen
Musei
Museos

TROPENMUSEUM

PUBLIC PARK and FOOTPATHS
Publiek Park en Voetpad
Jardin Public et Sentiers
Öffentliche Parkanlage und Fusspad
Giardino Pubblico dei Sentiero
Parque Publico y Senda

CEMETERY
Begraafplaats
Cimetière
Friedhöfe
Cimiteri
Cementerio

OUTDOOR STATUES and SCULPTURES
Standbeelden en Beeldhouwkunst buiten
Statues et Sculptures dehors
Im Freien stehende Standbilder und Skulpturen
Statue e Sculture all'aperto
Estatura y Escultura al fresco

Het
Lieverdje •

THEATRES and CONCERT HALLS
Theaters en Concertzalen
Théâtres et Salles de Concerts
Theater und Konzertsäle
Teatri e Sale dei Concerti
Teatros y Salas de Concertos

KONINKLIJK ■
THEATRE CARRÉ

CINEMA
Bioscoop
Cinéma
Kino
Cinema
Cine

TUSCHINSKI ■

RESTAURANT, CAFE or BAR
Restaurant, Café of Buffet
Restaurant, Café ou Bar
Restaurant, Cafe oder Bar
Ristorante, Cafe o Bar
Restorant, Cafe o Bar

Vlieghen ●

CABARET
Cabaret
Cabaret
Kabarett
Cabaret
Cabaret

MADAME ■

RAILWAY STATION
Station
Gares
Bahnhof
Stazione
Estación

CENTRAAL
STATION

MARKET
Markt
Marché
Markt
Mercato
Mercado

M

TOILET
Retirade Toilette Toilet Toeletta Retrete

WC

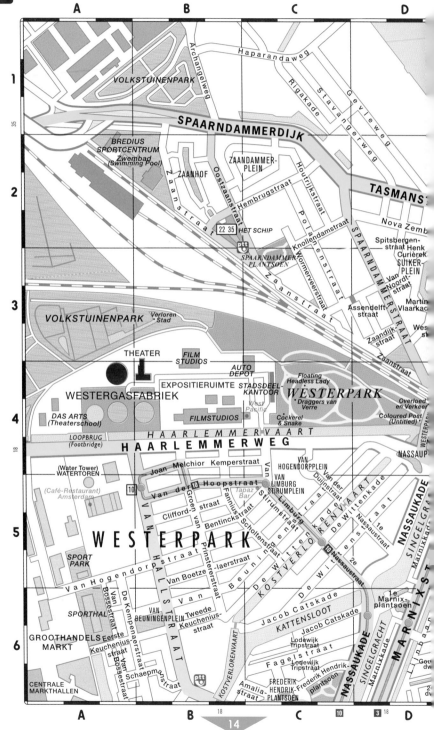

12

A   B   C   D

Haparandaweg

VOLKSTUINENPARK

Archangelweg

Rigakade

Stavangerweg

Gevleweg

SPAARNDAMMERDIJK

TASMANS

BREDIUS
SPORTCENTRUM
Zwembad
(Swimming Pool)

ZAANHOF

ZAANDAMMER-
PLEIN

Zaanstraa

Oostzaanstraat

Hembrugstraat

Houtrijkstraat

Nova Zemb

22 35 HET SCHIP

Knollendamstraat

Wormerveerstraat

Po

enstraat

Spitsbergen-
straat Henk
Curièrek

SUIKER-
PLEIN

SPAARNDAMMER
PLANTSOEN

Van
Noordt-
straat

Assendelft
straat

Martin
Vlaarkac

Zaanstraat

Zaandijk-
straat

Wes
st

VOLKSTUINENPARK

Verloren
·Stad

SPAARNDAMMERSTRAAT

Zaanstraat

THEATER

FILM
STUDIOS

AUTO
DEPOT

Floating
Headless Lady

Overloed
en Verkeer

WESTERGASFABRIEK

EXPOSITIERUIMTE

STADSDEEL-
KANTOOR

·Draggers van
Verre

WESTERPARK

DAS ARTS
(Theaterschool)

FILMSTUDIOS

West
Pacific

Cockerel
& Snake

Coloured Post
(Untitled)·

WESTERP

HAARLEMMERVAART

LOOPBRUG
(Footbridge)

HAARLEMMERWEG

NASSAUP

(Water Tower)
WATERTOREN

Joan Melchior Kemperstraat

VAN
HOGENDORPPLEIN

(Café-Restaurant)
Amsterdam

10 Hoopstraat

VAN DER

VAN
LIMBURG
STIRUMPLEIN

Van der
Duijnstraat

NASSAUKADE

Van der

Groen van

Tapaz
Bar

Limburg

De Wittenkade

1e

Clifford straat

Fannius

Scholtenstraat

Stirumstraat

Nassaustraat

1e

2e

W E S T E R P A R K

Bentinckstraat

Prinsterer

Beuning

2e

Nassaustraat

SPORT
PARK

HALLSTRAAT

Van Boetze

-laerstraat

KOSTVERLO

De Wit

1e
Marnix-
plantsoen

SPORTHAL

Van Hogendorpstraat

Van
Bossestraat

VAN
BEUNINGENPLEIN

Tweede
Keuchenius-
straat

Jacob Catskade

Jacob Catskade

GROOTHANDELS
MARKT

De Kempenaerstraat

Eerste
Keuchenius-
straat

KATTENSLOOT

Lodewijk
Tripstraat

Schaepm

KOSTVERLORENVAART

Amalia-
straat

FREDERIK
HENDRIK-
PLANTSOEN

Lodewijk
Tripstraat

Fagelstraat

Frederik Hendrik-
plantsoen

Singelgracht

NASSAUKADE

Marnixkade

Gou

SINGELS

M A R N I X S

CENTRALE
MARKTHALLEN

A   B   C   D

14

10

3 18

E F G H

39E 39E

UTHAVEN

DISTELWEGVEER

Distelweg

Grasweg

Klaverweg

39E

1

H E T

OUDE
HOUTHAVEN

E T

AMSTERDAM
NOORD

39E

2

HET VEEM
THEATER

GEBOUW
Y TECH

Van Diemenstraat

Roggeveenstraat Van
Dirk
Hartoghstr. Van Necks-
Van Linschoten- straat
Heemskerckstr. straat

**BARENTS-
PLEIN**

Barentszstraat

Bokking-
hangen

STENENHOOFD

I J

3

ZOUTKEETSGRACHT

Vierwindenstraat

Vierwinden-
dwars-
straat

Taan-
dwars-
straat

*De Gouden
Reael*

Zandhoek

Realengracht

R E A L E N G R A C H T

G O U D E N

R E A E L

WESTERDOKSDIJK

WESTERDOK

J

4

Galgen-
straat

Prinseneiland

Prinseneiland

Bickersgracht

Bickersstraat

Touws-
lagerstr.

Hollandse
Tuin

Westerdoksdijk

HAVEN
VOOR DE BINNEN
SCHEEPVAART

2e
leeuwers-
str.

Sloter-
dijkstr.

Nieuwe teertuinen

PRINSEN-
EILANDSGRACHT

Grote
Zeilmaker-
straat

HENDRIK
JONKERPLEIN

Blok-
maker-
str.
Ketelmaker-
straat

PB

5

1MER

MER

THE
MOVIES

HAARLEMMER HOUTTUINEN

EILANDSGRACHT

Westerdoksdijk

Wester-
dokskade

KAMER VAN
KOOPHANDEL
(CHAMBER OF COMMERCE)

18
17

16
15

DE RUIJTERKADE

brug-
steeg

Binnen

Dommers

Moutgan-
steeg

Buiten

Oranjestraat

Binnen

Vinken-
dijk

Buiten

NIEUWE WESTERDOKSTRAAT

Haarlemmer
Houttuinen
Buiten

Droogbak

14

13 12

OUWERSGRACHT

sstraat

ploem-
emstraat
traa

1e Gom-
dwarsstr.

KORTE PRINSENGRACHT

Thijssen
Theo
Thijssen

Haarlemmer

Posthoornkerk
(Offices)

Café Du
H

Anchor.
Binnen

Brouwersstraat

WEST
INDISCH
HUIS

HEREN-
MARKT

HOGESCHOOL VAN
AMSTERDAM

IBIS

CENTRAAL
STATION

GRACHT

Papeneiland
Bordewijk

Noordermarkt

Café
Tabac

NOORDERKERK

M

PRINSENGRACHT

BROUWERSGRACHT

Blemmerstraat

6

18

A B C D

1

CENTRALE
MARKTHALLEN

WESTELIJK MARKTKANAAL

De Schaepmanstraat
Van Bossestraat
Van Rappardstraat
Donker Curtiusstraat

VAN HALLSTRAAT

1e Kostverlorenkade
KOSTVERLORENSTR.
Kostverlorenstr.

Amaliastraat
Gerard Schaepstraat
Fred. Hendrikpl.

FREDERIK HENDRIK-PLANTSOEN

FREDERIK

HENDRIK-

Droombeeld (Vision)

W E S T E R P A R K

GROOTHANDELS MARKT

Buijskade

KOSTVERLORENVAART

Visseringstraat

Zaagmolenstraat

Frederik Hendrikplantsoen

PLANTSOEN

VAN OLDEN-BARNEVELDTPLEIN

2

van Ledenberchstr.
Hogerbeetsstraat

Gillis

1e Hugo det Grootstraat

Rombout

FREDERIK HENDRIKSTRAAT

Van Olden-

Barneveldtstraat

NASSAUKADE

SINGELGRACHT

Marnixstr.

MARNIXSTR.

21 80 82 89

3

JAN VAN GALENSTRAAT

2e HUGO DE

Marcantilaan

Kop van Jut

KOSTVERLORENVAART

Geuzenkade

3e Hugo de Grootstr.

Van Reigersbergenstraat

Van Houweningenstraat

HUGO DE GROOT-PLEIN

GROOTSTR.

FREDERIK HENDRIKSTRAAT

2e MARNIX-PLANTSOEN

Man met Vioolkist

4

Hugo de

Grootkade

GROOTGRACHT

Da Costakade

NASSAUKADE

SINGELGRACHT

BILDERDIJKPARK

Bilderdijkpark

PB

LIJNBAANSGRACHT

EBEN HAEZER
(YOUTH HOSTEL)

Bloe

13 14

Rozens

Lau

5

2e Kostverlorenkade

Elisabeth Wolffstraat

DE CLERCQSTRAAT

FREDERIK HENDRIKSTRAAT

DE CLERCQSTRAAT

12 13 14

VROOM & DREESMANN

Ter Haarstraat

Da Costastraat

DA COSTAGRACHT

Da Costastraat

DA COSTA-PLEIN

Allard

Pierson-straat

SINGELGRACHT

10 17 20

(BIKE HIRE)
MACBIKE

MARNIXSTRAAT

LIJNBAANSGRACH

12 13 14

6

Korte Blekersstraat
Agatha Dekenstraat
Schimmelstraat
Jan Hanzenstraat

Elisabeth Wolffstraat

Van Alphenstraat

BELLAMY-PLEIN

BILDERDIJKGRACHT

Bilderdijkkade

BILDERDIJKSTRAAT

KWAKERS-PLEIN

Kwakersstraat

STADSDEEL-KANTOOR OUED-WEST

POTGIETERSTRAAT

Costastraat

P

80 82 89 145
170 171 172 197
BUSSTATION

KINKERSTRAAT

7 17

PB

HOOFDBUR VAN POL

A B C D

3 12

7 17

145 1

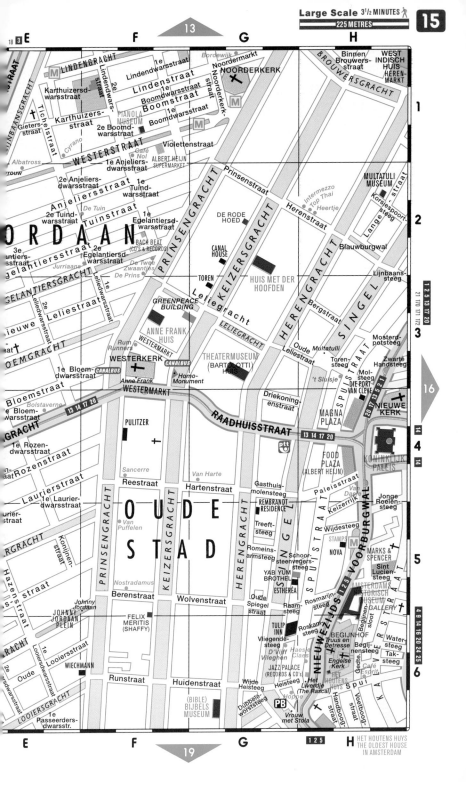

13
18 22   35

FREE FERRY TO
AMSTERDAM-NOORD

A   **B**   **C**   **D**

WEST
INDISCH
HUIS
HERENMARKT

Buiten
Vissers-
str.
Binnen
Wieringer-
straat
Binnen
Vissers-
straat

HOGESCHOOL VAN
AMSTERDAM

IBIS

BROUWERSGRACHT

Gouwenaars-
steeg

Stationsplein

CENTRAAL
STATION

DE

NEW YORK

Roomolenstr.

MULTATULI

OIBIBIO

Smak-
steeg

STROMARKT

NIEUWENDIJK

PRINS

HAVEN

STATIONS-
PLEIN

Centraal
Station

1

OUDE STAT

HERENGRACHT

Langestraat

Jeroenen-
steeg

Ronde
Lutherse
Kerk

RENAISSANCE

Koggestraat

KATTENGAT

Teerketelsteeg

HEKELVELD

MARTELAARSGRACHT

Ramskooi

HOLIDAY INN
CROWNE PLAZA

Nieuwezijds

Hasselaers-
steeg

Haringpak-
kerssteeg

VICTORIA

PRINS HENDRIKKADE

CANALBUS

FRONT

BARBIZON
PALACE

Sint
Olofspoort

PRINS HENDRIKKADE

FRANCE

SINT
NICOLAAS
(Media)
SCHREI

TRAM
1 2 5
17 13 20

TRAM
4 9 16
20 24 25

BUS TERMIN

18 21 22 28 32 34
92 94 100 104 106
112 114 117 122 1

STINGEL

SPUISTRAAT

NIEUWEZIJDS VOORBURGWAL

NIEUWE

DAMRAK

ZEEDIJK

OUDEZIJDS KOLK

OUDEZIJDS VOORBURGWAL

GELDERSEKADE

(Cat Boat)
DE POEZEN-
BOOT

Korsjespoort-
steeg

Korte
Korsjespoortsteeg

Korte
Kolksteeg

ROOMS
KATHOLIEK

SINT
NICOLAAS

AVENUE

DE KOLK

Nieuwezijds
Kolk

Sint Jacobsstraat

SEX
MUSEUM
TORTURE
MUSEUM

Karnemelk-
steeg

Kolk-
steeg

Armsteeg

Nieuwe
Brugsteeg

Wijngaards-
straatje

Guldehandsteeg

CENTRUM

Oudezijds

COK
CITY

2

Lijnbaans-
steeg

Korte
Lijnbaans-
steeg

Dirk Van Hasselts-
steeg

Suikerbak-
kersteeg

Manden-
makers-
steeg

Oude
Brugsteeg

Armsteeg

KABUL
PB

Heintje
Hoekssteeg

Elleboog-
steeg

ROYAL
KABUL

CITADEL
PB

20 17 13 2

Nieuwe Nieuwstraat

Onze Lieve
Vrouwsteeg

St. Geertruiden-
steeg

Sint Nicolaasstraat

Mosterd-
potsteeg

BEURS
VAN BERLAGE

Lange
Niezel

CROWN

Casablanca
VREDEN
burgersteeg

Waterpoort-
steeg

WA
EILAND

Kromme
Waal

3

15

21 170 171 172

Zwarte
Handsteeg

Blaeu-
straat

Gravenstraat

Eggert-
straat

NIEUWE
KERK
MOZES EN

TULIP INN
De Piserii

BEURS-
PASSAGE

AMERICAN
EXPRESS

Zout-
steeg

Damrak-
steeg

C&A

BEURS
PLEIN

Fontein

WINSTON

EFFECTEN
BEURS
(STOCK EXCHANGE)

BEURSSTRAAT

WARMOESSTRAAT

DAMRAK

Central MUSEUM
AMSTELKRING

Enge
Kerksteeg

Wijde
Kerksteeg

OUDEKERKS
PLEIN

Sint
Annenstraat

Korte-
Niezel

Korte
Storm-
steeg

Storm-
steeg

CASA
ROSSO

EROTIC
MUSEUM

OUDE KERK

OUDEKERKS
PLEIN

Kreupel-
steeg

BANANENBAR

Molen-
steeg

MARIONETTEN
THEATER

Bantammerstraat

Nieuwe

Binnen

Bredero

Brugsteeg

DE

WALLEN

SWISSOTEL
ASCOT

ptt

Valkensteeg

Nationaal
Monument

DAM

DE
BIJENKORF

GRAND HOTEL
KRASNAPOLSKY

Hermie-
tienstraat

RHO

DAMSTRAAT

Pillsteeg

Servetsteeg

Leidekkerssteeg

Sint
Jansstraat

Stoot
steeg

Kruispost

Monniken-
straat

(15c Weigh House)
WAAG
In de
Wag

Barndesteeg

Bloedstraat

Brande-
winsteeg

Nieuwe

RECHT BOOMS

RIDDER

Jastagewe

KONINGSSTRAAT

4

20 13 14 17

KONINKLIJK
PALEIS

Jonge
Roelen-
steeg

MAJOOR-STR.

Papenbroeks-
steeg

MADAME
TUSSAUD

PALEISTRAAT

Spaarpot-
steeg

Nadorst-
steeg

Pieter-
Jacobszstr.

Prinsenhof-
steeg

GRAND
Waalse
Kerk

Koestraat

NIEUW-
MARKT

Café
Cuba

ANTIQUES

Nieuwmarkt

M

5

1 2 5

KALVERSTRAAT

ROKIN

Gasper-
steeg

BRAKKE GROND

GERSTEKORREL

Steen-
houwerssteeg

St. Pieters-
poort-
steeg

St. Pieters-
halfsteeg

Enge
Lombardsteeg

OUDEZIJDS ACHTERBURGWAL

OUDE
DOELEN-
STRAAT

Bethanienstraat

OOSTINDISCH
HUIS

(1605)

Stoofsteeg

OUDE
HOOGSTRAAT

KLOVENIERSBURGWAL

PB

(1662)
TRIPENHUIS

ptt

NIEUWE
HOOGSTRAAT

SINT
ANTONIESBREESTRAAT

Dijkstraat

J.B.
Siebbeleshof

KROM.-BOOMS

Keizers-
straat

Korte
Dijkstraat

KONIN

Keizersstraat

Snoekjes-
steeg

OUDESCH

Sint
Lucien-
steeg

ENGE KAPELSTEEG

Duifjes-
steeg

Pilaar

CORDIAL

Celle-
broers-
steeg

Sint
Barberenstr.

FRASCATI

St.
Agnieten-
straat

Spinhuissteeg

Zanddwars-
straat
Zand-

ZUIDER
KERK
(1603)

Modder-
molenstraat

(1671)
PINTOHUIS

Deportatie
Column

Houtkoopers-
burgwal

REMBRANDT

Uitenpura

Van
Tin

6

WIJDE KAPELSTEEG

Stande

Waterstee

COSMIC End

ENGELSE

P.G.C. HAJENIUS
(CIGARS)

DE
Lange-
brugsteeg

Gebed
Zonder
End

Grimburgwal

Kuipers-
steeg

SAS ROYAL
RUSLAND

Slijkstraat

GROENBURGWAL

Ververstraat

ZWANENBURGWAL

WATERLOO
PLEIN

HOLLAND
EXPERIENCE

Houtkoopers-
dwarsstraat

JODENBREESTRA

DI

Mozes e
Aaronke

FLEA
MARKET

M

Taksteeg

Spui

Koningin
Wilhelmina

Oude Turfmarkt

ALLARD
PIERSON
MUSEUM

BOOKS

Vendelstraat

Oudemanhuis-
poort

Trees
with Lens

De
Engelbewaarder

Binnengasthuis-
straat

RAAMGRACHT

STADHUIS &
MUZIEKTHEATER
STOPERA

Olieslagers-
steeg

Nieuwe
Doelenstraat

Staalstraat

MAISON DE
BONNETERIE   **A**   4 9 14 16 20 24 25   **B**   **C**   20   **D**

DE WALLEN IS THE RED LIGHT DISTRICT

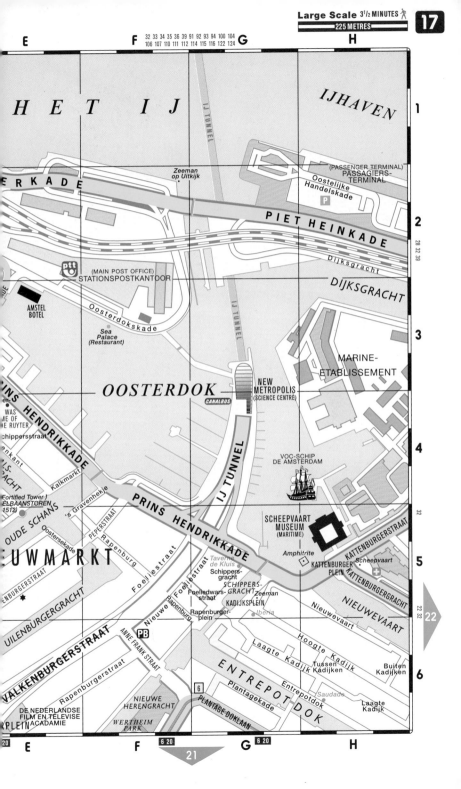

E   F   32 33 34 35 36 39 91 92 93 94 100 104   G   H
106 107 110 111 112 114 115 116 122 124

H E T   I J

IJHAVEN

1

ERKADE

Zeeman
op Uitkijk

(PASSENGER TERMINAL)
PASSAGIERS-
TERMINAL
Oostelijke
Handelskade
P

PIET HEINKADE

2

28 32 39

Dijksgracht

ptt
STATIONSPOSTKANTOOR
(MAIN POST OFFICE)

DIJKSGRACHT

AMSTEL
BOTEL

Oosterdokskade

Sea
Palace
(Restaurant)

3

MARINE-
ETABLISSEMENT

OOSTERDOK

NEW
METROPOLIS
(SCIENCE CENTRE)
CANALBUS

IJ TUNNEL

RINS HENDRIKKADE

WAS
ME OF
HE RUYTER
chippersstraat

VOC-SCHIP
DE AMSTERDAM

4

32

nkant

L.S.
GRACHT

Fortified Tower)
ELBAANSTOREN
1512)

Kalkmarkt

's Gravenhekie

PRINS HENDRIKKADE

SCHEEPVAART
MUSEUM
(MARITIME)

KATTENBURGERSTRAAT

OUDE SCHANS

Oostersekade

PEPERSTRAAT

Rapenburg

Amphitrite

KATTENBURGER
PLEIN
Scheepvaart

5

UWMARKT

Foeliestraat

Taverne
de Kluis
Schippers-
gracht

SCHIPPERS-
GRACHT
Zeeman

KATTENBURGERGRACHT

NIEUWEVAART

NBURGERGRACHT

Nieuwe

Rapenburg

Foeliestraat

Foeliedwars-
straat
KADIJKSPLEIN
Rapenburger-
plein
Iberia

Nieuwevaart

22 32

22

UILENBURGERGRACHT

ANNE FRANK STRAAT

PB

Hoogte Kadijk

Laagte Kadijk

Tussen
Kadijken

Buiten
Kadijken

6

VALKENBURGERSTRAAT

Rapenburgerstraat

Rapenburgerstraat

NIEUWE
HERENGRACHT

6

PLANTAGE DOKLAAN

Plantagekade

ENTREPOT-DOK

Entrepotdok

Saudade

Laagte
Kadijk

PLEIN

DE NEDERLANDSE
FILM EN TELEVISE
ACADAMIE

WERTHEIM
PARK

20   E   F   6 20   G   6 20   H

21

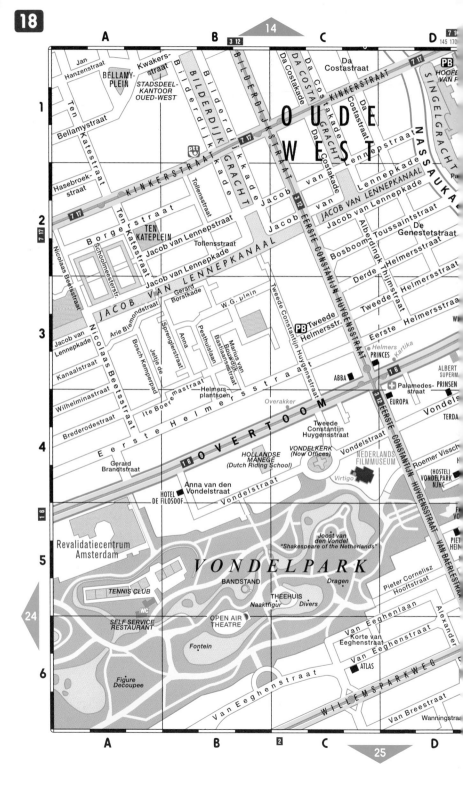

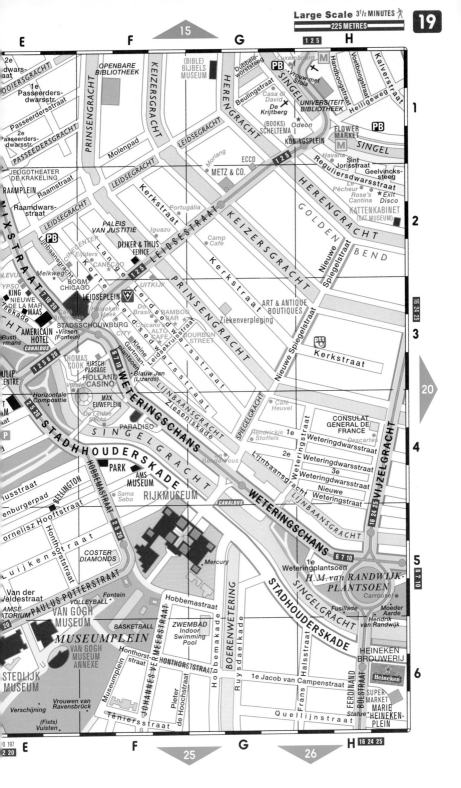

4 9 14 16 20 24 25 **A**   **B**   16   **C**   **D**

GROENBURGWAL   ZWANENBURGWAL

1

Kalverstraat
ROKIN
ROKIN
Oude Turfmarkt
ALLARD PIERSON MUSEUM
Vendelstraat
Binnengast- huisstraat
Doelenstr.
Staalstraat
VERVERS- STRAAT
WATERLOO- PLEIN
FLEA MARKET

Olies- lagersteeg
MAISON DE BONNETERIE
Café de Jaren
Nieuwe
Doelen
NES
Staalkade
STADHUIS & MUZIEKTHEATER
STOPERA
(TOWN HALL & THEATRE)

Heilige weg
VROOM & DREESMANN
UNIVERSITEITS- THEATER
Dantzig

PB
Roxy★
HOTEL DE L'EUROPE
HALVEMAANS- BRUG
BINNENAMSTEL
WATERLOO- PLEIN

MUNTTOREN (1619)
MUNTPLEIN
A m s t e l
ARCAM

SINGEL
DE KLEINE KOMEDIE
MONOPOLE
Balk in 't Oogsteeg
EDEN
Waterloo

FLOWER MARKET
PATHE DE MUNT
Regulies- steeg
Halvemaan-
Café De Kroon
Paarden- straat
Wagen- straat
Vive la Vie
Alfama

Geelvinckx- steeg
JOLLY CARLTON
REGULIERSBREESTRAAT
Escape
Bakker- straat
AMSTELSTRAAT
B 14 20

Reguliersdwars- straat
Schapen- steeg
4 9 14 20
MUSEUM WILLET-HOLTHUYSEN
It Disco
BLAUWBRUG (BLUE BRIDGE)

★Exit Disco
TUSCHINSKI
REMBRANDT- PLEIN
★Rembrandt

2

Peking
Reguliersdwarsstraat
Café Schiller
HERENGRACHT
BINNENAMSTEL
AMSTE

CANAL CROWN
THORBECKEPLEIN
SCHILLER
IMPERIAL
't Seepaard

ABN- AMRO BANK
ART MARKET
Thorbecke★
MADAME
DE ADMIRAAL

3

MUSEUM FODOR
HERENGRACHT
Sluizer
Quartier Latin
ptt

SEVEN BRIDGES
ARMADA
KEIZERSGRACHT
(SKINNY BRIDGE) MAGERE

KEIZERSGRACHT
CONCERTO (CDs & Records)
Kerkstraat
BRUG

MUSEUM VAN LOON
Café Krom
KONIN THEATRE

Kerkstraat
ORLANDO
PB
PRINSENGRACHT

Zinc.... et les dames
(Market Crier) De Markt Omroeper
Café Marcella
AMSTELSL (SLUICE GA

4

(17th century) AMSTELKERK
PRINSENGRACHT
Café Kort
Kekadorus
DE HARMONIE
PRINSENHOF
DE MUNCK

Noorderdwars- straat
(TRAVEL GUIDES) A LA CARTE
Backstage
ACHTERGRACHT

ARTHUR FROMMER MERCURE
De Duif Kerk
Annapurna

Noorderstraat
Nieuwe Looierdwars- straat
Utrechtsedwarsstraat

Nieuwe Looiersstraat
FREDERIKSPLEIN
Maarten Jansz. Kosterstraat

Fokke Simonszstraat
FALCKSTRAAT
Pillar
FREDRIKS- PLEIN

5

LIJNBAANSGRACHT
Fontein
SARPHATISTRAAT
6 7 1

WETERINGSCHANS
6 7 10

H.M. van RANDWIJK- PLANTSOEN
Eerste Wetering- plantsoen
NICOLAAS WITSEN
NEDERLANDSCHE BANK
OOSTEINDE
Achter Oosteinde

Hendrik M. van Randwijk
Den Texstraat
WESTEINDE
Sarphatik

16 24 25
ASTERISK
Nicolaas Witsenstraat
Pieter Pauwstraat
Huidekoperstraat
SINGELGR

Nicolaas Witsenkade
SINGELGRACHT
STADHOUDERSKADE

6

HEINEKEN BROUWERIJ
STADHOUDERSKADE
Hemonylaan
Hemony- Flinckstra

★Heineken
Van WOUSTRAAT
Goverf

SUPERMARKET
MARIE HEINEKEN- PLEIN
1e Van der Helststraat
2e Jacob van Campenstraat
HABITAT
Gerard Doustraat
Nicolaas Berchemstraat
Albert Cuypstraat
Twe Jan Ste

26

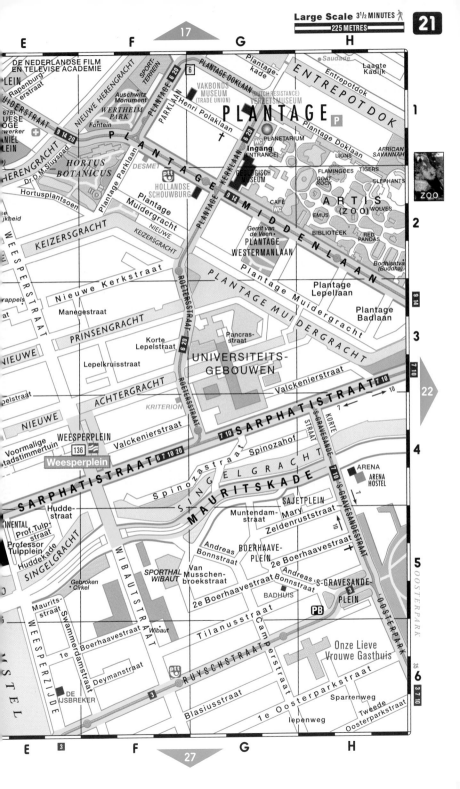

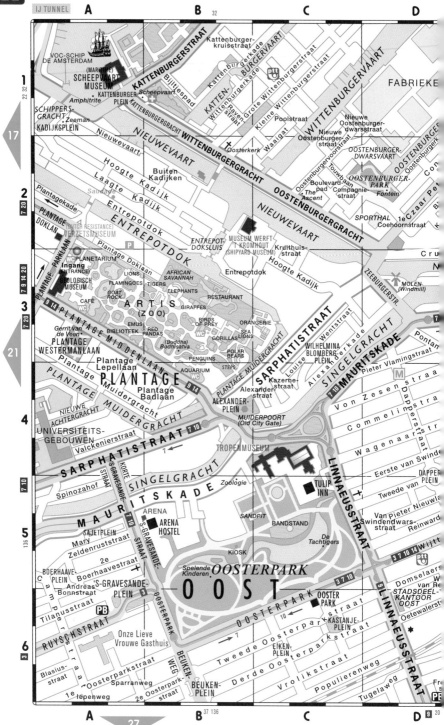

A   B 32   C   D

22 32

17

7 20

7 9 14 20

21

7 10

136

VOC-SCHIP
DE AMSTERDAM

(MARITIEM)
SCHEEPVAART
MUSEUM

KATTENBURGERSTRAAT

Kattenburger-
kruisstraat

BURGERVAART

KATTENBURGERGRACHT

WITTENBURGERGRACHT

Kattenburger KATTENBURGER
PLEIN

Amphitrite

Scheepvaart

Bijltjespad

Kattenburgergracht

Raven-
straat

KATTEN-
Wittenburgergracht

Grote Wittenburgerstraat

Kleine Wittenburgerstraat

WITTENBURGERVAART

FABRIEKE

SCHIPPERS-
GRACHT

Zeeman

KADIJKSPLEIN

Nieuwevaart

Oosterkerk

Waalgat

Poolstraat

Nieuwe
Oostenburger-
straat

Nieuwe
Oostenburger-
dwarsstraat

OOSTENBURGER-
DWARSVAART

OOSTENBURGER-

Plantagekade

Hoogte Kadijk

Buiten
Kadijken

NIEUWEVAART

OOSTENBURGERGRACHT

Oostenburgervoorstraat

Touwbaan

OOSTENBURGER-
PARK

Boulevard
The
Ascent

Compagnie-
straat

Fontein

1e Czaar Pet

PLANTAGE
DOKLAN

Sauduna

Laagte Kadijk

ENTREPOTDOK

NIEUWEVAART

SPORTHAL
Coehoornstraat

(DUTCH RESISTANCE)
VERZETSMUSEUM

Plantage Doklaan

ENTREPOT-
DOKSLUIS

MUSEUM WERFT
'T KROMHOUT
(SHIPYARD MUSEUM)

Kruithuis-
straat

ZEEBURGERKADE

PLANETARIUM

Ingang
(ENTRANCE)

ZOOLOGISCH
MUSEUM

LIONS

AFRICAN
SAVANNAH

Hoogte Kadijk

Entrepotdok

MOLEN
(Windmill)

Cr u
N

CAFÉ

GOAT
ROCK

TIGERS

ELEPHANTS

RESTAURANT

Wentstraat

7

ARTIS
(ZOO)

EMUS

BIBLIOTEEK

RED
PANDAS

GIRAFFES

BIRDS
OF PREY

ORANGERIE

GORILLAS

SEA
LIONS

SARPHATISTRAAT

Louise

Wilhelmina
Blomberr-
Plein

SINGELGRACHT

Pontan

Gerrit van
de Veen

PLANTAGE
WESTERMANLAAN

(Buddha)
Bodhisatva

PENGUINS

POLAR
BEARS

STEPS

Plantage Muidergracht

Alexanderkade

MAURITSKADE

Pieter Vlamingstraat

PLANTAGE MIDDENLAAN

Plantage Lepellaan

PLANTAGE
Plantage
Badlaan

AQUARIUM
WC

Alexander-
straat

Kazerne-
straat

Von Zesenstraa

Dapperstraa

NIEUWE
ACHTERGRACHT

PLANTAGE Muidergracht

ALEXANDER-
PLEIN

MUIDERPOORT
(Old City Gate)

Commelinstr

Wagenaarstr

UNIVERSITEITS-
GEBOUWEN

SARPHATISTRAAT

Valckenierstraat

7

TROPENMUSEUM

Eerste van Swinde

DAPPER
PLEIN

Spinozahof

SINGELGRACHT

Zoölogie

TULIP
INN

Tweede van
Swindendwars-
straat

Reinward

MAURITSKADE

ARENA

Mary
Zeldenruststraat

ARENA
HOSTEL

SANDPIT

BANDSTAND

KIOSK

De
Tachtigers

LINNAEUSSTRAAT

Van pieter Nieuwl

Wijtt

Domselaers

W
van Re

SAJETPLEIN

2e

BOERHAAVE
PLEIN

Boerhaavestraat

Andreas
Bonnstraat

'S-GRAVESANDE-
PLEIN

Spelende
Kinderen

OOSTERPARK

OOST

OOSTER
PARK

STADSDEEL-
KANTOOR
OOST

Oetewalerst

Tilanusstraat

RUYSCHSTRAAT

Onze Lieve
Vrouwe Gasthuis

OOSTERPARK

KASTANJE-
PLEIN

10

EIKEN-
PLEIN

straat

Blasius-
straat

Oosterparkstraat

Sparranweg

Tweede Oosterparkstraat

Derde Oosterparkstraat

Vrolikstraat

Populierenweg

Tugelaweg

Fr
s

1e Iepenweg

2e Oosterpark-
straat

BEUKEN-
PLEIN

BEUKEN
WEG

E 32 32 F 32 39 59 G H

Panamakade
SPOORWEGBASSIN PIET HEINTUNNEL

PIET HEINTUNNEL **Z E E B U R G** 1

Borneolaan Borneolaan F. de Boerstraat

Panama- Borneokade
straat

Borneolaan

ENTREPOTHAVEN 2

Jaap
Haanis
ENTREPOTBRUG
Entrepotkade Zeeburgerkade CRUQUIUSWEG 22

**STADSDEEL-
KANTOOR
ZEEBURG** HET NEDERLANDS
PERSMUSEUM
(PRESS MUSEUM) HILDO
KROPPLEIN
Boulevard
Café Cruquiusweg J. M. v.d. Meylaan

Veemarkt H.A.J.Baanderskade

Veemarkt Veemarkt Veemarkt

NIEUWEVAART **NIEUWEVAART**

Zeeburgerpad Zeeburgerpad

rpad **L O Z I N G S K A N A A L**

Z E E B U R G E R D I J K 3

7 10 **Billiart** Kramatweg

TIMOR-
PLEIN Timorstr. Lombokstr Billiton-
straat Menado-
straat Ternate-
straat Kramatweg

Delistraat Padangstr. Dlambistr. Soenda-
straat N i a s s t r a a t Karimata-
straat

Bankastraat Madurastraat Makassar- Boetonstraat Bawean-
straat

Madurastraat Javastraat Het Java- **J A V A S T R A A T** JAVA-
PLANTSOEN
Balistraat Balistraat PB Eerste Atjehstraat 1e
Ceramstraat 14
37
Eerste Atjehstraat CERAMPLEIN 2e
Ceramstraat
Tweede Atjehstraat Riouwstraat Haroekoestraat

Riouwstraat **I N S U L I N D E W E G** 14

**MUIDERPOORT
STATION** 7 10 14 7 Soerabaja- Bataviastraat Preanger- Mataram-
straat straat 5
Moskee Batavia
OOSTER-
POORTPLEIN 3 15 22 37 Palembang- Solostraat **ISRAËLITISCHE
BEGRAAFPLAATS**
(CEMETERY)
39 59 66 straat OBIPLEIN Tidorestraat
120 126 Formosa- AMBON- SUMATRA-
PLANTSOEN
Ter straat PLEIN
Gouwstraat BONI- Boni- Batjan-
PLEIN straat straat Sumatrastraat
Siboga- Sumatrastraat
straat
Valentijnkade **R I N G V A A R T** 6
66

**VOLKSTUINENPARK
FRANKENDAEL**
(ALLOTMENTS)
SPORTHAL **R I N G V A A R T**

E F 15 66 G H

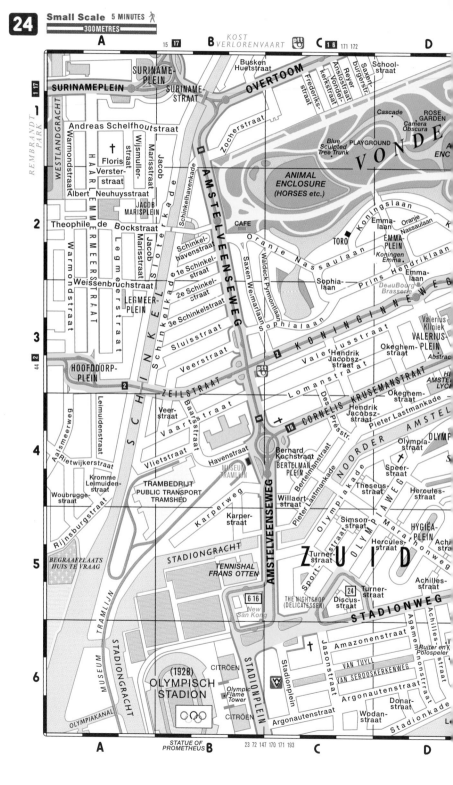

A   15 **17**   B *KOST VERLORENVAART* ptt   C **1 6** 171 172   D

1 17

REMBRANDT PARK

SURINAME-PLEIN

SURINAMEPLEIN

SURINAME-STRAAT

Busken Huetstraat

OVERTOOM

Frederiks-straat

Anslostraat

Vondel-kerkstraat

Reyer Anslostraat

Saxer-burgerstr.

School-straat

Zocherstraat

Cascade

V O N D E

ROSE GARDEN

Camera Obscura

1

WESTLANDSTRAAT

Warmondstraat

Andreas Schelfhoutstraat

Wijsmuller-straat

Jacob Marisstraat

✝ Floris Verster-straat

Blue Sculpted Tree Trunk

PLAYGROUND

ENC

Albert Neuhuysstraat

JACOB MARISPLEIN

Schinkelhavenkade

ANIMAL ENCLOSURE (HORSES etc.)

HAARLEMMERMEER

2

Warmondstraat

Legmeerstraat

Theophile de Bockstraat

Jacob Marisstraat

Weissenbruchstraat

Schinkel-havenstraat

1e Schinkel-straat

2e Schinkel-straat

CAFE

Oranje Nassaulaan

TORO ◼

Koningslaan

Emma-laan

Oranje Nassaulaan

EMMA-PLEIN

Koningen Emma

Emma-laan

Hendriklaan

LEGMEER-PLEIN

3e Schinkelstraat

Saxen Weimarlaan

Waldeck Pyrmontlaan

Sophia-laan

Prins Hendrik-laan

Emma-laan

DeauBourg Brasserie

3

HOOFDDORP-PLEIN

Schinkelkade

Sluisstraat

Veerstraat

Sophialaan

Valeriusstraat

Vale riusstraat

Hendrik Jacobsz-straat at

Okeghem-straat

VALERIUS-PLEIN

Valerius Kliniek

Abstrac

44 **2**

SCHINKEL

2

ZEILSTRAAT

Lomanstraat

Des Presstr.

CORNELIS KRUSEMANSTRAAT

Hendrik Jacobsz-straat

Okeghem-straat

HI AMSTE LYC

4

Aalsmeerweg

Leimuidenstraat

Rietwijkerstraat

Veer-straat

Vaarstraat

Baarsstraat

Vlietstraat

Havenstraat

Bernard Kochstraat

✝

Bertelmanstraat

16

Bertelman-PLEIN

NOORDER

Pieter Lastmankade

AMSTEL

OLYMP

Olympia-straat

Speer-straat

Hercules-straat

AMSTELVEENSEWEG

Woubrugge-straat

Kromme Leimuiden-straat

TRAMBEDRIJT PUBLIC TRANSPORT TRAMSHED

MUSEUM TRAMLIJN

Willaert-straat

Pieter Lastmankade

Olympiakade

Theseus-straat

Marathonweg

5

Rijnsburgstraat

BEGRAAFPLAATS HUIS TE VRAAG

Karperweg

Karper-straat

STADIONGRACHT

TENNISHAL FRANS OTTEN

Z U I D

Turner-straat

Sportstraat

Simson-straat

Hercules-straat

Achillesstraat

HYGIËA-PLEIN

Achi stra

TRAMLIJN

STADIONGRACHT

MUSEUM

6 16

New San Kong

THE NIGHTSHOP (DELICATESSEN)

Discus-straat

24

Turner-straat

Achilles-straat

STADIONWEG

6

OLYMPIAKANAL

(1928) OLYMPISCH STADION ⬤⬤⬤

CITRÖEN

Olympic Flame Tower

CITRÖEN

STADIONPLEIN

STADIONPLEIN

Jasonstraat

✝

Amazonenstraat

VAN TUYL

VAN SEROOSKERKENWEG

Argonautenstraat

Argonautenstraat

Ruiter en K Polospeler

Agamemnonstraat

Donar-straat

Wodan-straat

Achilles-

STADIONKADE

A   *STATUE OF PROMETHEUS* B   23 72 147 170 171 193   C   D

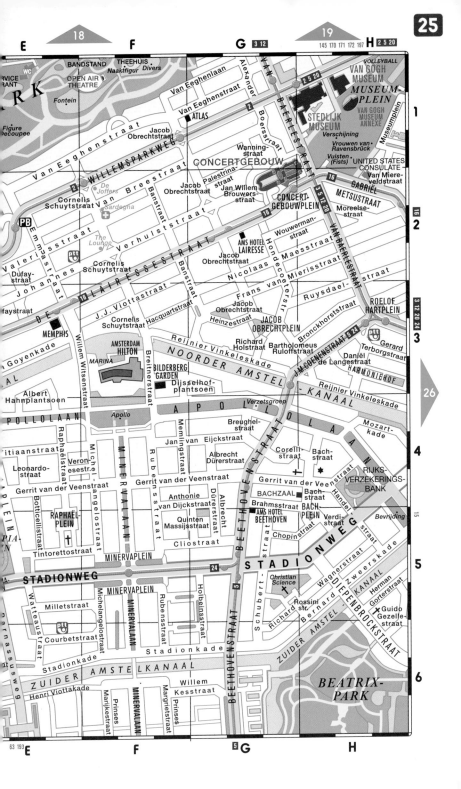

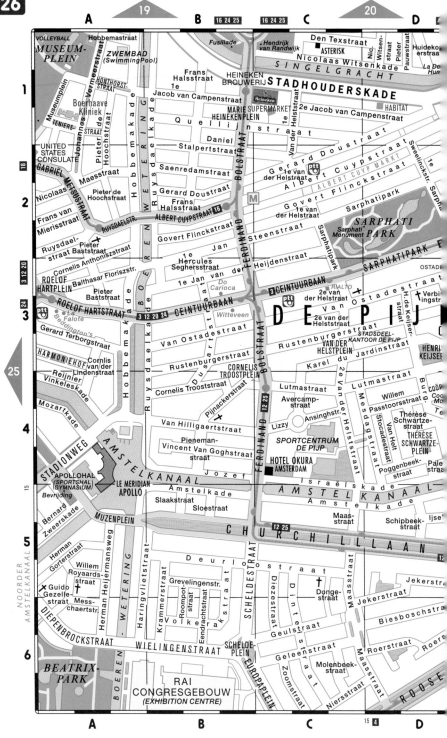

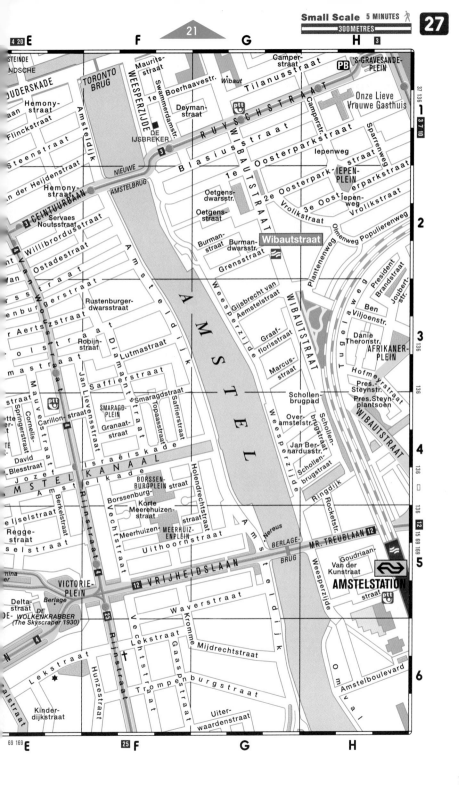

4 20 E   F   G   H 3

STEINDE
NDSCHE

Maurits-
straat

Camper-
straat

's-GRAVESANDE-
PLEIN

PB

TORONTO
BRUG

Swammerdamstr.

1e

Boerhaavestr. Wibaut

Tilanusstraat

Onze Lieve
Vrouwe Gasthuis

Hemony-
laan

Deyman-
straat

Campersfr.

1

37 136

3 7 10

Flinckstraat

DE
IJSBREKER

Blasiusstraat

1e Oosterparkstraat

Iepenweg

Sparrenweg

straat

Steenstraat

NIEUWE

AMSTELBRUG

2e Oosterpark-
straat

IEPEN-
PLEIN

erparkstraat

n der Heijdenstraat

Oetgens-
dwarsstr.

3e Oost Iepen-
weg

Vrolikstraat

Hemony-
straat

CEINTUURBAAN

Oetgens-
straat

Vrolikstraat

Olnenweg Populierenweg

2

136

Servaes
Noutsstraat

Burman-
straat

Burman-
dwarsstr.

Wibautstraat

Plantenenweg

President
Brandtstraat

Joubert-
str.

Willibrordusstraat

Grensstraat

Ostadestraat

Gijsbrecht van
Aemstelstraat

Ben
Viljoenstr.

Rustenburger-
dwarsstraat

Graaf-
florisstraat

Danie
Theronstr.

AFRIKANER-
PLEIN

3

136

r Aertszstraat

Robijn-
straat

Lutmastraat

Marcus-
straat

Hofmeyrstraat

Pres.-
Steynstr.

136

Saffierstraat

Schollen-
brugpad

Pres.Steyn
plantsoen

Carillon straat

Smaragd-
straat

Over-
amstelstr.

WIBAUTSTRAAT

4

136

Cornelis-
Springerstraat

SMARAGD-
PLEIN

Granaat-
straat

Topaasstraade

Jan Ber-
nardusstr.

Schollen-
brugstraat

David
Blesstraat

Israëlskade

Holendrechtstraat

Schollen-
brugstraat

Ringdijk Rocketstr.

136

MSTEL

KANAAL

elkade

Vechtstraat

BORSSEN-
BURGPLEIN straat

MR. TREUBLAAN

12

12 15 69 169

e Ijselstraat

Berkelstraat

Borssenburg-

Korte
Meerehuizen-
straat

Nereus

BERLAGE-

BRUG

AMSTELSTATION

5

Regge-
straat

selstraat

Meerhuizen-

MEERHUIZ-
ENPLEIN

Uithoornstraat

Goudriaan-
Van der
Kunstraat

PB

VICTORIE-
PLEIN

12

VRIJHEIDSLAAN

straat

Delta-
straat
DE-
WOLKENKRABBER
(The Skyscraper 1930)

Berlage

25

Waverstraat

6

Kromme
Lekstraat

Mijdrechtstraat

Amstelboulevard

Hunzestraat

Trompenburgstraat

Gaaspestraat

Uiter-
waardenstraat

Kinder-
dijkstraat

SERVICES AND USEFUL INFORMATION

Information Centres

AMSTERDAM TOURIST OFFICES
Inside Centraal Station (Platform 2)	**C1 16**
Opposite Centraal Station	**C2 16**
Leidsestraat	**F3 19**
Stadionplein	**C6 24**

The above Offices are open Daily.
At Schipol Airport:

HOLLAND TOURIST INFORMATION
is open from 7.00 - 22.00.
Telephone Information ☎ *0900 400 40 40*
From abroad dial ☎ *31 6 340 340 66*

Emergency Services

POLICE - AMBULANCE - FIRE Dial *112*
Main Police Station **D6 14**
Elandsgracht 117. ☎ *5599111*

MEDICAL SERVICES
For Doctor - Dentist - Chemist ☎ *5923434*

HOSPITALS WITH EMERGENCY ROOMS
Andreas Ziekenhuis
Theophile de Bockstraat 8. ☎ *5111115*
Vu Ziekenhuis
De Boelelaan 1117. ☎ *4444444*
Sint Lucas Andreas Ziekenhuis
Jan Tooropstraat 164. ☎ *5108911*
Onze Lieve Vrouwe Gasthuis **H6 21**
's Gravesandeplein 16. ☎ *5999111*
Slotervaartziekenhuis
Louwesweg 6. ☎ *5129333*

LOST PROPERTY
The Police Lost and Found office is located at:
Waterlooplein 11. **D1 20**
Open Mons to Fris 11.00 - 15.00 ☎ *559 8085*
Articles lost on Public Transport
Prins Hendrikkade 108-114. **F5 17**
Open Mons to Fris 09.00 - 16.00 ☎ *551 4911*

PHARMACIES
Monday to Friday 09.00 - 17.30.   After closing
☎ *694 87 09* to find the late night Pharmacy.

POST OFFICES
Central Post Office 🏤 **G4 15**
Singel 250-256. Open Mons to Fris 09,00-18.00
Thurs until 21.00, Sats 10.00-13.30.
Other offices are open 09.00 - 17.00.
Stamps can also be purchased from tobacco shops.
A 24-hour service for long-distance telephone
calls and telegrams is available at the
Telehouse Raadhuisstraat 48-50. **G4 15**

TELEPHONE To make an Intenational call dial 00
then dial the Country Code - United Kingdom 44,
USA & Canada 1, Ireland 353, Australia 61, then
the Area Code followed by the individual number.
Directory Enquiries ☎ *06 8008*
International Enquiries ☎ *06 0418*
*Most Call Boxes take Phonecards which can be
bought at Post Offices and the Tourist Offices.*

BANKING HOURS Banks open from 9.00 to
16.00 from Monday to Friday. You can change
money at the Tourist Office (no commission) or
at Post Offices as well as at a Bank.

TRAMS Most of the tramlines run from Centraal
Station. They start at 6.20 and finish just after
midnight. There are some night buses that run at
either 30 or 60 minute intervals (see back cover).
Tickets for use on trams, buses and the metro can
be bought in strips of 2 to 45: two strips are for

one zone; most tourists will only need the large
Centrum zone. When buying tickets on a tram
tell the driver the number of zones and how many
persons are using the ticket and he will stamp
your ticket. For other trips you insert your ticket
in the yellow stamping machine (at the rear of
the tram or near the platform stairs on the Metro)
*Tickets are valied for one hour and can be used
on connecting Trams, Buses or Metro in that time.
Tickets can also be bought from the Tourist Offices.*
TAXIS Taxis cannot be hailed, but there are many
taxi ranks located throughout the city, otherwise
telephone *677 77 77.*

Bicycle Hire

Around Centraal Station there are many Bike Hire
firms usually requiring a deposit and your passport
Always lock the bike and never ride two-abreas
- it is illegal - and remember that you have the
tram tracks to negotiate as well if you are not a
regular cyclist. See also MACBIKE (D5 14).

Canal Cruises

There are many cruises to choose from; most
start opposite or near Centraal Station and there
is no doubt this is an excellent way to acquaint
yourself with the city. There are brunch, tea and
candlelight dinner cruises to choose from; one
such cruise is run by:
LOVERS
Prins Hendrikkade opposite 25-27 near the Station.
This company also runs a trip to ARTIS Zoo.
CANAL TAXIS
You can hail these from the canalside and then
travel anywhere you wish to go. ☎ *62 221 81*
CANAL-BUS
This firm operates a hop on, hop off line - most
of the stops are indicated on the maps in this
atlas with the symbol: **CANALBUS**
CANAL-BIKE
These are for the energetic. They are four seater
pedal boats with four moorings: Rijkmuseum,
Leidseplein, Keizergracht and Anne Frank Huis.
You hire at one of these and leave at one of
the other moorings.

CLOTHING and SHOE SIZES approximate						
SHIRTS						
Europe	36	37	38	39	40	41	42
UK and USA	14	14.5	15	15.5	16	16.5	17
DRESSES						
Europe	36	38	40	42	44	46	48
UK	8	10	12	14	16	18	20
USA	6	8	10	12	14	16	18
MEN'S SHOES						
Europe	39	40	41	42	43	44	45
UK and USA	6	7	7.5	8.5	9	10	11
WOMEN'S SHOES						
Europe	35.5	36	36.5	37	37.5	38	39
UK	3	3.5	4	4.5	5	5.5	6
USA	4.5	5	5.5	6	6.5	7	7.5

DRUGS are illegal in Holland. Anybody found
with cocaine and heroin can expect prosecution.
The attitude to marijuana and cannabis is to
turn a blind eye to it when it is sold and smoked
in the so-called coffee shops.

INDEX TO STREETS

INDEX NOTES   *The letters following a name indicate the Square and Page Number*

Hoogte - Higher	Binnen - Inner	Eerste (1e) - First
Tussen - Middle	Buiten - Outer	Tweede (2e) - Second
Laagte - Lower	Straatje - Alley	Derde (3e) - Third

In the Dutch Language IJ is the equivalent of Y and follows in that sequence

Copyright © MICHAEL GRAHAM PUBLICATIONS 1999

Thanks to Lien van der Kooi (Pathé Cinemas), Mark Weemen Fotograaf, the Rijksmuseum, Anne Frank House, the Philadephia Museum of Art, the Rembrandt House Museum, and the Van Gogh Museum for permission to use their works

Cover and Page 1 Illustrations
by Ronald Maddox PRI, FCSD.

PENGUIN BOOKS

First Published 1999
1 2 3 4 5 6 7 8 9 10

Published by the Penguin Group
Penguin Books Ltd, 27 Wrights Lane, London W8 5TZ, England
Penguin Putnam Inc., 375 Hudson Street, New York, New York 10014, USA
Penguin Books Australia Ltd, Ringwood, Victoria, Australia
Penguin Books Canada Ltd, 10 Alcorn Avenue, Toronto, Ontario, Canada M4V 3B2
Penguin Books (NZ) Ltd, Private Bag, 102902, NSMC, Auckland 10, New Zealand
Penguin Books Ltd, Registered Offices: Harmondsworth, Middlesex, England

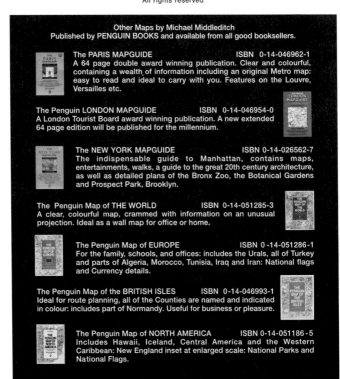